Your Outta Control Cat

Christine Church

For Candy
(September 1983 - August 2003)
A cat who was hardly ever outta control.
Thank you for 20 wonderful years of companionship.

T.F.H. Publications, Inc.
One TFH Plaza
Third and Union Avenues
Neptune City, NJ 07753

This book has been published with the intent to provide accurate and authoritative information in regard to the subject matter within. While every precaution has been taken in preparation of this book, the publisher and author assume no responsibility for errors or omissions. Neither is any liability assumed for damages resulting from the use of the information herein.

Library of Congress Cataloging-in-Publication Data
Church, Christine.
Your outta control cat / Christine Church.
p. cm.
Includes index.
ISBN 0-7938-2902-X
1. Cats-Behavior. 2. Cats-Training. I. Title
SF446.5 .C57 2003
636.8--dc22
2003017177

Printed and bound in USA

www.tfhpublications.com

Contents

How Did My Cat Turn Into a Monster?

A re you living with an out of control cat? Cat owners often wonder what's gotten into their feline companions when they misbehave. The sound of claws ripping through your furniture is like fingernails being dragged across a chalkboard. Your cute little kitten tears through the house, runs over the table of expensive collectibles, and climbs up your designer curtains. How about that puddle on your expensive Persian carpet?

Where did you go wrong? Perhaps nowhere. Bad, or "monster," behaviors can come from a variety of sources. Some are learned, and others are instinctual. Some are not "bad behaviors" but are just different from what humans might term acceptable. You, as your cat's caretaker, need to learn the solutions to prevent bad behaviors that are

In addition to being knowledgeable about general feline issues, a cat owner should pay close attention to his cat's specific behaviors.

new or are not yet ingrained, retrain those that are present, and accept and understand those behaviors that make your cat...well, a cat.

The trick to understanding your cat's unruly behavior is to first learn and understand feline behavior, then to understand your own cat's individual nuances. It may not be that your cat has turned into a monster, it just may seem that way until you understand why your cat is misbehaving and learn how these problem behaviors can be modified.

This book will help you solve unwanted feline behaviors with maximum effectiveness. Everything from clawing furniture to litter box habits will be explained, so sit back and relax, and prepare to be dazzled by the feline psyche.

Profile of an Outta Control Kitten

Kittens learn most of their adult behaviors from mom while they are still very young. Sometimes behavioral problems can manifest at a very young age if the mother was not a very good teacher, if junior was not a good student or if he was taken away from mom too soon. Kittens are at their most impressionable during their first eight to ten weeks of life, and often, behaviors developed or begun at this age become permanent.

A Kitten's Life

The events in a typical day for a litter of kittens are guiding factors in how the kittens grow and what they learn. While their eyes are still closed, mom does just about everything for her children. The most prominent instinctual behavior at this age is the ability to find food (in this case, one of mom's teats). Mom does the bathing and cleans up after their wastes. All this early cleanliness is the beginning of the fastidious cat and can be traced back to its wild ancestry.

After their eyes open, the kittens begin to wander around and learn new behaviors, such as defecating away from the nest. Before the kittens are

Cleanliness is one of the most important lessons a kitten can learn from his mother.

How Did My Cat Turn Into a Monster?

Some of a kitten's behaviors are instinctual, reinforced by his mother and later by his owner.

weaned (at around four weeks of age), most kittens are taught how to bury their feces (a behavior that, in the wild, would help prevent the young from being detected by predators), hunt (which is generally in the form of mock fighting and play amongst siblings), bathe themselves and one another (for cleanliness, another behavior which helps keep them safe and undetectable), and defend themselves. Often, these behaviors are instinctual acts reinforced by mom's teachings.

If the mother cat is lazy (and this does happen with some cats), abandons her babies, or if the babies are taken away from her too soon, some learned behaviors might go unfinished. For instance, if mom is lax in teaching a kitten how to bury his waste, the end result can sometimes produce a cat that does not bury his waste. The cat might only go on top of the litter and walk away, or make a half-hearted attempt at burying the waste. In some cases, the cat may avoid the litter box occasionally or even altogether.

The good news is that most cats have at least some instinctual knowledge that tells them to bury their waste, or in the very least, to go on a soft, shiftable surface (such as dirt or sand). Much of the litter box etiquette is still taught by mom. A litter box deficiency doesn't always point to mom's bad example, however. Often there is a cause beyond what was learned or not learned in the nest. Litter box difficulties are

Your Outta Control Cat

the number one reason cats are given up to shelters and there are numerous reasons for this behavioral problem.

Adolescence, a.k.a. Temporary Insanity

Though early life is by far the most important time in a kitten's developmental and learning processes, not all behavioral problems start in the nest. Like people, cats develop their own

personalities as they grow, and some behaviors seem to manifest right along with the growing up process. This is where we come to the adolescent cat, the time generally between the ages of 6 to 18 months.

The most common reason for a cat to be given away is a litter box problem.

It can be a very difficult time period. Often, human parents become frustrated and want to tear their hair out, or wonder where they went wrong and try to figure out what they can do to guide this seemingly misguided youth into becoming a well-formed adult cat.

Adolescence in cats is not all that different from adolescence in humans, and being the guardian of an adolescent cat can be just as frustrating. This is the time when many people think, "Did I make a mistake in acquiring this cat?" Suddenly that cute little kitten climbing the drapes or running up your body as if you were a tree isn't so cute anymore. This is the time when many cats are sent back to wherever they came from or end up in shelters. This is also a time that, fortunately, is only temporary. Most cats leave adolescence around one year of age, some a bit earlier, and others don't seem to "grow up" until they are one and a half years old. Often, it depends on the breed, or just on the cat.

Most adolescent cats, similar to adolescent humans, will be very curious.

Your Outta Control Cat

Hormones are the cause of many behavioral patterns in your adolescent cat.

Adolescence is a time marked by insecurities and experimentation, just like with a teenaged human. And, as with human teenagers, it a time marked by hormones. This accounts for much of an adolescent cat's behavior patterns. Your happy indoor kitten might suddenly decide that roaming outside would be fun, and develop a fascination with the door and make a dash for it every time it opens. The kitten that was too small to jump on the counters now can...and does. Your ankles and pant legs become prime attack targets. Your female cat is going into heat, yowling at all hours, and driving everyone batty. Your male cat is spraying on the walls. And how about all those claw marks on your furniture?

The adolescent cat, just like the kitten, is still prone to environmental suggestion and the attitudes of those around him. For example, if a cat at this age is shooed out of the room every time company comes in the door,

How Did My Cat Turn Into a Monster?

Teach the Rules

Most cats are good at obeying the rules of the house if they are taught correctly, persistently, and consistently by everyone in the household. For example, if one person never allows the cat to jump on the counter, and another person in the house does, the cat will become confused and never understand fully what is expected of him.

that cat will develop a fear of people coming in the door.

This is also the best training time for the owner to teach the cat the rules of the house. They say that you can't teach an old dog new tricks; well, teaching an old cat new tricks is even harder. Being persistent in your training of the adolescent cat will lead to a GCC (Good Citizen Cat) who knows the rules.

Adolescent Behaviors

Adolescent cats are learning their boundaries, experimenting with territory, and testing the waters, so to speak. They will also test your patience at times. Certain adolescent behaviors that need to be nipped in the bud right off include spraying (which can usually be solved by getting your cat fixed at or before six months of age), aggressions (which will be discussed in chapter two), and predatory behaviors, which are normal. What you need to do is create an outlet for your kitty's instincts. Adolescent cats have a lot of pent-up energy. Play with your cat every day and use a variation of interactive toys. Feather toys are great for playing chase and jump. String can also be chased, and is even more entertaining with a toy mouse tied to one end. Just make sure your cat doesn't swallow the string or it can cause major problems.

Young cats (and even older ones) have what are known as "energy spurts" at odd hours. These often occur early in the morning or late at night. If you are an early riser, this shouldn't pose a problem, but for many who are awakened by the sound of cat feet tearing through the

Your Outta Control Cat

house, this can be frustrating. Try engaging your early riser in a heavy play session and a late-night snack before bed. With many cats, this will hold them over until morning. Usually this behavior settles down as a cat ages. My cats, who are all over eight years of age, still have their energy spurts, but usually at reasonable hours.

When a Cat is Just Being a Cat

Sometimes what is construed as a behavioral problem by the cat owner is merely a cat doing what comes naturally. In other words, your cat is just being a cat. In order to understand and correct true behavioral problems, it's important to learn the difference between the abnormal and the normal.

It is also important to remember that your cat may be trying to tell you something with his behavior, and he is not trying to spite you or drive you crazy (though at times it might seem that way). But cats, just like people, have needs, desires, and wants. So how is a cat, which does not speak your language, supposed to communicate his dissatisfaction to you? He does it the only way he knows how— through behavior.

Some behaviors are natural, and unless a cat has been trained to

Consistency is a very important part of teaching your cat the rules of the house.

How Did My Cat Turn Into a Monster?

Your Outta Control Senior or Disabled Cat

Youth is not the only time period in which a cat might be considered "outta control." Old age can cause health related issues that can manifest into annoying behaviors. Older cats can become incontinent, or their minds may not be what they used to, and therefore cause the cat to behave in new and unexpected ways.

If you adopt an older cat, you might be faced with the result of a previous owner's mistreatment, or a cat that has been allowed to misbehave for so long that the "bad" behavior has become ingrained and natural. This is much harder to deal with and correct, but it can be done.

Disabled cats can produce their own set of pathologies. Blind cats need to have familiar surroundings at all times or they will run into the furniture. Similar issues reside for deaf cats. They will not be able to hear you call them, and you will need to train your cat to respond to a signal, such as the lights flicking on and off.

understand what is expected of him in the home, he will continue to act out his natural desires. For example, cats love to view the world from a high vantage point. Therefore, they will climb (and need to climb, instinctually) whatever is available to get to that point, whether it is the counters or the drapes.

Home environment also plays a big role in the way your cat behaves. Does your cat go outside? Outdoor cats and indoor cats usually will develop in very different ways. Apartment cats, living in smaller spaces with less room to run around, can develop lazy habits or become destructive due to lack of activity. Regardless of the situation, if a cat's needs are not being met, physically or mentally, he will find ways of showing his displeasure or frustration.

Sometimes the only explanation for feline behavior is that your cat is just being a cat.

How Did My Cat Turn Into a Monster?

Cats love to climb and will often use whatever means are available to get them to a higher level.

What Else Can I Do?

No matter what the behavior problem is, the first step to help determine a cure is through a physical examination. Many problems, particularly urinary deficiencies, can be caused by or started due to a physical malady. For example, if your cat is exposed to an unpleasant situation and associates the litter box with it, the cat may start to avoid the litter box. If you notice that your kitty starts to exhibit a new and inappropriate behavior, make an appointment with the veterinarian immediately. Your vet should know your cat as well as you do. A complete physical will help the vet determine the best course of action for your cat's treatment. Barring that, keep reading this book. Most behavior problems can be solved with patience, knowledge, and perseverance.

Clues to Your Cat's Behavior

In This Chapter You'll Learn:

✳ How to deal with fear behavior

✳ What to do about territorial aggression

✳ How to combat loneliness and boredom in your cat

✳ What to do if your cat is stressed

P icture this scenario: You have just moved into a new house and the previous owners had cats. You only have one very well-behaved kitty that has never missed his mark when using the litter box and has never placed a claw on anything other than the cat scratching post. However, within a week of moving into this house, your precious kitty sudden turns Mr. Hyde on you. He is urinating on the wall-to-wall carpeting, spraying on the walls, and scratching the molding. What happened?

The previous owners' cats left their mark behind. "But the house was scrubbed from top to bottom," you say. Perhaps it was, but that wall-to-wall carpeting is the same and your kitty has a great deal of olfactory nerves, making his sense of smell highly acute. He can smell

Sometimes the solution to your cat's behavior problems might not be very obvious.

the marks those other kitties made, and now he wants to claim this territory for his own. Even neutered cats can spray, particularly in a new environment where other cats have lived. Your cat has to make this house his home, too. And in cat sense, that is how he does it.

In the above scenario, the answer to your cat's sudden bad behavior is obvious, but in another scenario it might not be so apparent. That's why it is up to the owner to do a bit of investigation work if your cat suddenly acts out of character.

Playing Sherlock Holmes

So how do you go about investigating your cat's behavior and finding where the problem lies? And once you do discover the problem, how do you go about fixing it? The first thing to ask yourself is, what has changed in my cat's environment?

Very often, bad behaviors start as a result of a drastic, or even subtle change in the cat's routine or environment. Cats are creatures of habit. They need consistency in their lives to be happy. Some cats, if acclimated to be on the move constantly from a young age (such as show cats), are more accepting of change in their lives, but even they need certain constants. All cats do. It gives them security, and if a cat's sense of security is threatened, his behavior will often change for the worse. Sometimes a change that is so subtle to us that we can scarcely notice it is drastic enough for your cat to be thrown off kilter.

Has a new cat been hanging around the neighborhood? I have seen the most relaxed and well-behaved housecats become utter monsters when a strange cat started hanging about outside. The situation is worse if your cat goes outside and gets into scraps with this new cat. Housecats can become very frustrated and begin attacking you or spraying on the walls, clawing at the window, or yowling.

A cat will be affected by changes in the lives of those around him.

Clues to Your Cat's Behavior

How about your life? Do you have a new boyfriend or girlfriend? Have you recently divorced? Did one of the kids move out? Did another pet in the house, or a family member close to you pass on? Cats are sensitive creatures, and though they can't tell you what they feel inside, they do feel deeply and react to changes around them.

Fear Behaviors

Is your cat afraid? Fear occurs when a cat's sense of personal safety is threatened. A typically fearful cat might flatten his ears down onto his head, shrink back as if trying to appear smaller, and hiss. Some cats that are afraid will put on a front of audacity by fluffing up to appear larger, thus hoping to intimidate whatever is threatening their sense of safety. But being afraid isn't always an immediate response, and a scared cat might simply stay in hiding or develop behavioral problems that are removed from the actual fear (such as avoiding the litter box).

When a cat is scared, he will not always immediately exhibit signs of fear. He may choose to hide or act out in other ways that are unrelated to what initially caused the fear.

A variety of behavioral problems can be born through fear. If your cat is new to your house, fear (to some extent) is almost a given, though different cats will respond in different ways. A more outgoing and personable cat that has had good human socialization may show little or no fear, where a former feral cat might hide for months, and hiss at anyone who comes near. If your cat has had a traumatic experience, fear will often be the result, and can typically manifest into other behavioral problems that go beyond the symptoms of fear itself.

Fear is a normal part of a cat's adjustment to a new home. Take this into account as you try to help your new feline get over his anxiety.

For example, let's say you are afraid that your new kitten will get out of the house whenever anyone comes over. So, every time anyone walks in the door (even if it is the same person each day) you whisk the kitten off to another part of the house. Your kitty will grow to fear anyone coming into your house (with the exception of you, somehow they always know) and will develop a fear of strangers. Even if this behavior is changed later on, the behavior has been ingrained and will continue throughout the cat's life. Some cats might eventually start to come around if they see that the way is always safe when people come over, but almost all cats will retain some level of anxiety about strangers. And if it was your husband's arrival that always triggered your kitty's removal, she will develop a fear of your husband (particularly if he has little else to do with her).

Clues to Your Cat's Behavior

Identify the Fear

The first step in eliminating a cat's fear is to identify what is causing that fear. Sometimes the answer is obvious. If your cat hides whenever a child walks in the house, then you know that the cat has a fear of children. Other times, however, the answer might not be so obvious and may require a little detective work on your part. Is there a new cat in the area that your kitty is frightened of? Is there street construction somewhere your cat can hear (remember that cats can hear noises from much farther away than we can)? Is a child teasing your cat?

Once you figure out what is causing your cat to be afraid, work on eliminating the cause and then easing your cat's fear.

Once you've identified the problem, you have to eliminate it or avoid it and then work on alleviating your cat's fear. If a behavioral problem developed from that fear, you will then have to work on combating that problem.

Combating Fear

The way to go about modifying your cat's behavior will depend on what the fear is, what developed from it, and how severe it has become. We will discuss the most practical methods, since many people are not equipped with the time, space, or even ability to go into a complete modification program.

Your Outta Control Cat

If the fear is a mild one, exposing the cat slowly but continuously to the fear might help her to realize that nothing about it will harm her, as long as there is nothing to frighten her further. More severe fears will require time, patience, and retraining.

Since most cats love to eat, the most practical method of reconditioning your cat would be through food. Make his reward come in the form of small treats, or something the cat doesn't get often, and only give the cat small amounts. (You don't want a tubby tabby at the end of the training.)

You want your kitty to associate the treat with a positive, non-fearful situation. So begin by giving him the treats when all is calm and he is showing no signs of fear. Praise him and talk softly and kindly to him. After a time, he will come to associate that treat with feeling good. Once this happens, it is time to start slowly and gently exposing him to whatever is causing the fear. If he fears a person, you will have to find a room where the cat cannot run off and disappear, yet you don't want him to feel trapped, either.

Feed your kitty in his special place and then show him the treats. Have the person he is afraid of come into the room. This person should offer the

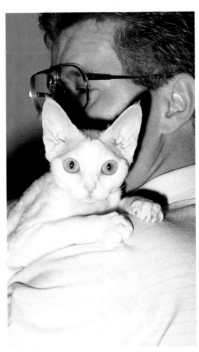

Different fears require different methods of treatment.

One of the most practical ways to help alleviate your cat's fear is to remind him how much you love him by spending time with him.

Your Outta Control Cat

treats your kitty has grown to love. If the cat still seems overly afraid, end the session and try again the next day. Continue to give the cat positive reinforcement. Eventually, the person might want to try petting the cat while he eats, or feeding him small amounts of butter from his or her finger. Try anything you can think of to give your kitty a positive outlook on the situation.

Other Fears

If you want your cat to accept riding in the car, you should try to start this at a young age, if possible. Again, positive reinforcement is the key. Use food and catnip toys to keep the cat distracted and happy while in the car. (Keep your cat in a travel crate at all times. Never allow a cat to ride loose in a car.) Have a passenger whom your kitty trusts sit with him and offer toys and treats through the crate door while you concentrate on driving.

If your cat fears another cat or other animal, you can try feeding them together with a cage separator or with two people monitoring the situation (one person to control each animal). This is not feasible, however, if the other animal your cat fears is the neighbor's cat-hating dog. In a case like that, you will have to provide your cat a good escape route, or make him an indoor cat.

Cats like stability. If you want your cat to be willing to travel, start acclimating him to the idea early in life.

Clues to Your Cat's Behavior

In extreme cases, a cat might need the help of a veterinarian or a behavioral consultant to help him overcome his fears.

Aggressive Behaviors

Cats are natural predators. They are taught hunting maneuvers in the form of mock play from the time they are kittens. They will tumble with their littermates, bite, and often grab necks and kick with their hind feet. This is all normal behavior, and when your newly acquired kitten jumps out from behind the sofa to grab hold of your ankle, he is participating in an instinctual ritual that can be likened to a lion hiding in the brush, waiting to attack his unwary quarry. This is called play aggression and can be very cute when a tiny kitten attacks your feet moving about under the covers or bites your fingers when he wants attention or something to eat.

However, some play aggressions can become downright nasty or even dangerous if they are allowed to continue on through to adulthood. Those little needle-like teeth become fangs, and the kitten's tiny claws become talons. Of all the varying forms of aggression, play aggression is the least worrisome, and in most cases, the easiest to solve or

26

Aggressive behaviors are natural in your kitten, but should be under control by the time he is an adult.

prevent. As cute as some of these behaviors may be, unless you want your adult cat doing them, it's best to nip them in the bud from kittenhood. This is not too difficult for most play aggression behaviors. Your kitten will grow out of some of these behaviors and others might just be acceptable.

Behavioral Consultation

In severe cases, such as with rescued feral cats, you might want to enlist the aid of a behavioral consultant or veterinarian. Your vet might even recommend a medication to help calm your cat while you work on a behavioral modification routine.

These behavioral websites might help:

www.vetconsultantsonline.com/forms/vcofeline.doc

vetmedicine.about.com/library/diseases/blcat-behav.htm

Remember, some cats might never completely get over their fears.

Separating Good and Bad Fear

Separating good fear from bad fear can also help your cat. This will depend on your situation and the cat's environment. If your cat is strictly an indoor cat, then fearing the door or outside is a good fear. But if this fear has developed into behavioral problems, it has become a bad fear. Fear of cars for a cat that is allowed outside and goes into the road is a good thing, and can prevent the cat from running into the road when a car is coming. However, if your cat is so afraid of your car that he gets sick every time he needs to go to the vet, then that fear has become a bad fear. While an outdoor cat should fear and steer clear of strange dogs, you don't want your pet cat fearing your dog.

Learn to know which fears are "good" for your cat. Sometimes, in a light way, certain fears can be utilized in your cat's training or retraining. Never force fear into a cat or force a cat to do something he is deathly afraid of or you will have an even more neurotic cat on your hands.

Kittens are impressionable, and if you are consistent in teaching your kitten certain behaviors are unacceptable, chances are the behavior will disappear by the time he is an adult. The best way to teach your kitten what is unacceptable is to hiss in his face and say, "No!" in a harsh voice. If his claws are stuck in you, gently grab his paw and say, "No!" in his face while carefully pushing his paw away. These procedures are more effectual than waiting until the cat is an adult and the behavior is ingrained. If these corrections are carried out consistently, they should prove to be very successful.

Territorial Aggression

Besides play aggression, one of the most common forms of aggression is territorial aggression. This is when a cat is threatened by the presence of another cat or animal and feels he must defend his territory. This is all well and good until your beloved kitty comes home with tattered ears and a bloody nose, or your housecat starts hissing at everything that moves because a new cat in the neighborhood is hanging around outside.

Territorial aggression can also cause many problems within a multi-cat household. Although cats can learn to live in packs, and often form their own groups and hierarchies within the house, there are times when cats simply do not get along. This feline rivalry occurs when two or more cats in the same house can't walk past one another without a hiss or a swat, or the very least, a belligerent leer. The more cats that occupy a household (particularly an indoor-only household), the greater the chance of feline rivalry.

Cats are very protective of their territory. This can be especially disruptive when a cat and a kitten share a home.

Clues to Your Cat's Behavior

Causes of Feline Rivalry

There are many causes of feline rivalry. Generally, the older cats get the less likely they are to accept a new cat onto their territory. Kittens are easiest to place together, so if you plan to have more than one cat it is recommended to get two kittens of approximately the same age. An older cat and a kitten in the same house can often cause problems as the more active kitten will want to play and the older cat will just want to be left alone.

Feline rivalry can also be caused by scent. Cats have a very strong sense of smell. If your two kitties suddenly start hissing at one another after you move into a new house where other cats have lived, they are hissing

Sometimes cats who were once friendly with one another lose interest in the friendship or even become enemies. The most common cause of this shift is the addition of another cat into the household.

Your Outta Control Cat

Competition between cats is common with more than one living in a household.

because they can smell the previous cats and are upset by it. The house will have to be thoroughly disinfected (which it should be anyway, particularly if cats lived there). A cat that has recently come home from a stay at the veterinarian's office might not be welcomed with open paws by other cats in the household. He will smell like the vet hospital, and this is generally not a scent associated by cats as being a pleasant one. The other cats might hiss at him, swat at him, or otherwise reject him when he first comes home. This is temporary, and as he starts once again to take on the familiar odors of the household, everything should fall back into place as it once was.

Can't We All Just Get Along?

Just as not all people get along due to clashes in personality, so is true for cats. Some cats might just not like one another, particularly if they did not grow up together. The more cats that are present in the household, the higher the chance of personality clashes. Even slight changes in routine can upset the delicate balance of a group of cats within a house and spats can occur.

Clues to Your Cat's Behavior

It is normal for some cats to be the best of friends and others to be less friendly.

Competition can also cause squabbling. This can include competition for food, which is the most common, competition for owner attention, or competition for toys. It is natural to have spats in a multi-cat household every now and again. If one cat chooses to steal another's food or wants the catnip mouse the other is playing with, small tiffs can ensue. But these are nothing to be alarmed about and generally need no owner interference. Only if the competition gets out of hand should you do something about it.

Cats that have not been spayed or neutered (particularly two whole males) will fight it out if they are put together. They are trying to establish territory. If not neutered at a young age (by six months) male cats that once got along as kittens may become archenemies. Female cats in heat can cause a male cat to go wild in the house. He may spray urine and show aggression to other animals and humans.

Your Outta Control Cat

A female cat that has not been spayed by six months of age might seem to be the friendliest cat around at one moment, and then be clawing at your hand when you try to pet her the next. She will howl a lot and drive everyone in the house crazy. This type of aggression and behavioral problem is easily solved: make sure your kitty is spayed or neutered by six months of age. Up to 95 percent of the time, aggression and territorial spraying will be solved if your cat is fixed at a young age. The longer you wait, the longer the behavior has to ingrain in the cat's routine and psyche, and the higher the odds become that the cat will not stop the bad behavior even after being fixed.

Fear Aggression

Fear aggression is another common form of aggression that cats display. A frightened cat that is backed into a corner might puff up its fur to look larger, hiss, spit, and then lash out violently. He might crouch low, lay his ears back, and tuck his tail under his body. This behavior is

A frightened cat may try to protect himself by puffing up his fur. By making himself appear bigger, he hopes to scare off any danger.

Clues to Your Cat's Behavior

A certain amount of fear can help to keep your cat safe, but excessive fear is not healthy.

Remember to give all of your cats plenty of attention and love. This can eliminate many potential jealousy problems.

usually in response to a threat. The cat is ready to defend himself. Never grab a cat that looks like this, even if it is a cat that you know, or you could be very sorry. If you absolutely must get hold of this cat, throw a blanket over him, and carefully grab him into your arms and hold him tight to your body so he doesn't feel insecure being held out in the air. Get this cat into a secure carrier as soon as possible. It will not be easy to hold a cat that is in this state for long.

Displaced Aggression

Sometimes, particularly in a household with many cats, or in a cat colony where hierarchies are formed within the established groups, bully cats will pick on cats lower in ranks. Often, the bullied cat will go after another cat in the group much lower in rank. This is called displaced (or redirected) aggression. This can also happen when a cat is frustrated because he cannot take out his aggression on the source of his anger. For instance, if a housecat sees a dog or another cat that

Many cats will get jealous of a new addition to the family, whether human or animal. Allow time for the cat to adjust before becoming concerned.

he finds threatening out in the yard and wants to attack, he might instead attack another cat in the house or another animal in frustration.

Jealousy

Cats can feel jealous and sometimes a cat will show jealousy in the form of a behavioral problem such as urinating or defecating on his owner's belongings. Don't ignore your cat. Many people get a cat under the false notion that cats are completely self-sufficient and need no care other than some food and water thrown down once a day. If this is the case, then why bother? Get a cat statue or a painting. A real cat needs much more attention and love. They have feelings and emotions just as humans do, and they have their own way of showing their dissatisfactions. The trick is to know how to read and understand what it is the cat is trying to tell you, and to know what to do about it.

Jealousy is usually a fairly obvious emotion. If a new pet or a new child comes into the house, or if the owner's schedule changes to the point where it interferes with the cat's normal routine, jealousy can ensue.

Problem jealousy occurs when something causes the cat to feel insecure, such as a change in his environment or routine (which includes the loss of loved ones for whatever reason). Jealousy can then develop into behavioral problems, such as inappropriate urination or defecation. Cats have been known to urinate in suitcases or overnight bags if they know their owner will be going away and is leaving them alone. Some cats become aggressive when frustrated or jealous, or they scratch in places they know they are not supposed to (which is not the same as a cat who simply hasn't been taught the proper scratching place). Cats thrive on love and attention, and if a cat has grown accustomed to things being a certain way, he will be most upset if the routine changes.

Fighting among the cats of a household should be a rarity. If fights become commonplace, an effort should be made to end them.

Clues to Your Cat's Behavior

Sometimes one cat will steal another cat's food. If this is the case, try feeding your cats in different locations.

The most common cause of jealousy seen is when a new baby comes into the home. The cat is confused about this new little person who suddenly gets all the attention. He might hang around the child, eye this strange creature, or avoid it altogether. Either way, an appropriate introduction can help alleviate jealousy and problems.

Too Many Cats?

Overcrowding can cause many problems. Don't get more cats than the house can hold or than the other cats can handle. The number of cats you can have will depend on the size of your house, the age of the cats, and their personalities. Usually, one cat per room is a good number.

Solving Aggression Problems

Solving territorial disputes is not always easy and solving the problem will depend on what type of dispute is present and how severe it is. If it's simply a matter of competition, then feed the quarreling cats in different locations to prevent one from stealing the others' food. Make sure that each cat has plenty of

38

playtime, and plenty of tender loving care. Play is a great stress reducer and a cat that has had plenty of play interaction will be calmer, sleep better and be less likely to cause fights.

Fighting

There will always be tiffs in a household with many cats, but often these are small skirmishes that can work themselves out. If one cat simply

If one cat is bullying another, they should be separated, at least until they calm down.

Clues to Your Cat's Behavior

Try to correct your cat's behavioral problems while he is still young.

likes to swat at another as she walks by, or a slight hiss is voiced, ignore it. You should interfere only if it erupts into a continuous regime of fights. Don't grab at the quarreling cats. Instead, stomp your foot and holler, or spray some water from a spray bottle at them to stop the fight and make the cats separate.

If this fighting becomes a habit, particularly if one cat is getting hurt, something should be done to reinsert peace into the household. Sometimes it can be as simple as separating the fighting cats during the time when they would be most likely to quarrel. Feed them in different rooms if necessary. Sometimes a separate cat tree, or a taller cat tree with many tiers, can keep them from fighting over sleeping arrangements, as most cats like to sleep in the highest spot possible. You might want to try buying each cat his own bed, or making sure each cat has a special sleeping spot all his own. Getting them to use their beds is a matter of attracting each cat to his bed using a toy

Time-Outs

Keeping your cat busy is important. If he never has time to get bored or is kept satisfied with many activities, he will be less likely to develop behavioral problems in the first place. Time-outs can be very beneficial if two cats are fighting. Lock each cat in its own room for a short time until they both cool off.

Your Outta Control Cat

If your cats are fighting, give each cat his own special place to sleep.

Clues to Your Cat's Behavior

If changes in his family or his environment cause your cat to start misbehaving, it is likely because he feels left out. Try your best to make him feel secure and loved.

or catnip and making the area a positive place. After that, most cats will go there on their own to sleep.

Bullies

Bully cats are often born out of a house with too many cats of varying personalities and ages. If you have a cat that seems to be relentlessly bullying another cat in your house, separation is the key to peace. Sometimes, if space permits, this separation can be a permanent one or last until one of the cats calms down. Many times, finding the reason behind the bullying can help. In a case of redirected aggression when one cat is picking on another, and the insulted cat picks on yet another cat, the problem is with the first cat. The problem should be taken care of on that end. Again, separate feeding and sleeping spaces can work wonders.

The best time to curb aggressive behaviors is during kittenhood. It's cute when that little bundle attacks your ankles as you walk by or chews on your fingers. But any behavior that is encouraged ("Oh, how cute!")

Homemade Toys

With a little ingenuity and thought you can make toys for your cat at home without having to spend an arm and a leg on expensive toys that your cat will just ignore. However, be sure to keep safety in mind when making cat toys. Don't use anything your cat might chew off and swallow or become sick on. Common objects found around the house can be utilized for kitty's enjoyment. For example, bounce a small rubber ball or ping-pong ball and watch your cat's reaction. What about string? Drag a piece along the floor and watch your cat chase it. You can even make your own catnip toys with some cat-approved material (nothing treated with chemicals) and homegrown catnip.

will eventually become permanent, and unless it is a behavior you can live with as the cat ages, curb it in the beginning. When your kitten bites you, hiss in his face and set him down. Let him know that this is unacceptable behavior. As he ages, and if this unwanted behavior was never encouraged, your cat will eventually stop doing it. Once the kitten has grown into an adult, the behavior will be harder to modify.

Cat toys don't need to be expensive. Homemade toys, like a piece of string or a paper bag, can provide just as much entertainment for your cat.

Clues to Your Cat's Behavior

Emotional Stressors and Your Cat

The following is a list of emotional triggers that may cause your cat to feel stressed, thus possibly bringing on behavioral problems.

* Boredom/loneliness
* Competition for affection
* Death (human or animal)
* Feline rivalry
* Jealousy (of another human or animal)

Separation Anxiety

Separation anxiety is caused when one cat is separated from another cat, person, or even an environment that they have grown to love or be accustomed to. For example, if two cats were very close and one passes away, the other will often go through a period of feline mourning and can develop anxiety and even behavioral problems due to the grief of being separated from his friend.

Separation anxiety in itself is not usually cause for concern; it is the boredom, loneliness, and/or depression that accompanies it that can create turmoil for your cat. This turmoil can lead to behavior problems as the cat has no other way of showing and releasing its frustrations. Even moving from one location to another might cause a cat to feel separated and set apart, because he misses the environment with which he was so familiar.

Divorce or the death of a human the cat knew well can also cause separation anxiety. If a child moves away to college, the cat he or she played with or grew up with will feel left behind.

44

Like humans, cats are affected by stress. During especially stressful times, be sure to spend extra time playing with your cat.

Loneliness and Boredom

Loneliness can happen to an only-cat or to a cat that has lost a beloved companion (human or animal). A cat that is alone in the house is prone to developing what is known as the only-cat syndrome. If your cat has been left as an "only cat" for too long, often that cat will no longer

Environmental Stressors and Your Cat

The following is a list of things in your cat's environment that may cause him to feel stressed, thus possibly bringing on behavioral problems.

* ❋ Arrival of new family member, animal or human
* ❋ Confinement
* ❋ Crowding
* ❋ Lack of fresh air and sunshine
* ❋ Loud noises
* ❋ Moving to a new home

Spend plenty of time playing with your cat and showing him how much you love him. This will prevent loneliness and boredom, which can sometimes lead to destructive behavior.

Your Outta Control Cat

When your cat misbehaves, say, "No!" in a strong, firm tone of voice.

accept a new pet into the household. For some cats and cat owners, this arrangement is fine, as long as the owner recognizes that he or she is their cat's sole source of entertainment and companionship and makes sure that the cat receives the proper amount of attention, play, and love. But for the cat owner who is not home all day, two cats are actually better than one. They will entertain one another, play together, and bathe together.

A cat that is lonely will display various symptoms, including lethargy and the appearance of being down, not wanting to play, staring out the window, not eating, or destructive behavior.

Other cats might become aggressive if they are bored. In mock-play, they will leap out from a corner and attack your feet. Cats need interaction, and this behavior is just your cat seeing you as another cat to play with. Usually this is not a problem, particularly if it's only

Clues to Your Cat's Behavior

Sometimes the addition of a kitten to your household can help a bored cat by giving him a friend to play with.

occasionally or if you don't mind the intrusion. But if the cat begins to hurt you or others, or if the behavior is getting out of hand, then it is time to take action. In a case such as this, you will have to get to the root of the problem, which will be why your cat is bored or lonely to begin with. Is he experiencing a form of separation anxiety or is he grieving for the loss of a loved one?

Play and interaction with the cat owner is the best medicine. If your cat is young enough and accepting enough, another kitten to play with might be just the thing he needs. If not, then you should set up play times for you and your kitty pal.

The Stress Factor

Cats are creatures of routine and habit. When something in their world changes (such as a new family member moving into the home, getting a

Your Outta Control Cat

new pet, or moving), some cats become stressed. All cats handle stress in different ways, and some cats misbehave as a way to act out or vent their stress. Finding and eliminating the cause of the cat's stress is the first major step toward changing the cat's behavior, but there are other steps you can take to prevent or lessen your cat's level of stress.

Importance of play

If your cat appears "down" or is acting lethargic, stress of some sort may be the culprit. Get him moving. During stressful times, add extra playtimes with your cat. Regular play can also help keep stress from building up in the first place, barring

Space For Everyone

Make sure your cats have plenty of room to run and play, particularly young kittens that are often rambunctious. Crowding among cats can also cause stress, so enough room must be available for each cat's individual needs.

A lack of space can also be stressful for cats. Make sure every cat has enough room to comfortably move about and play.

How to Deal with Stress

If your cat is very upset, you might want to talk to your veterinarian about getting stress-reducing medications for your cat. These should only be used in severe cases, and temporarily while the problem is being worked on. Never give your cat over-the-counter medications or those intended for people or other animals unless directed by your vet to do so.

unusual circumstances, of course. Exercise can also help to keep your cat's weight down. Obesity may cause stress on the cat's body and cause the cat to become more lethargic and more vulnerable to stress.

Cats need interaction and regular play. Even older cats can benefit from play. My arthritic 20-year-old still plays if I draw a string around in front of her. Many cats, particularly younger cats, find their own games and

Cats love to play—with their toys, their owners, and other cats.

Your Outta Control Cat

Sometimes two cats are better than one. They can keep each other company and make up for any lack of human interaction.

make their own fun. Other cats need to be enticed. Catnip, bird feeders outside the windows, scratching trees, toys, and kitty greens are all essential elements to your cat's well-being. Make up games and experiment until you find which games your cat enjoys most, then set aside time each day to play these games. Some cats will enjoy obstacle courses to run, soap bubbles to chase or just a rolled up ball of foil to bat around. Cats seem to love paper balls. Interactive toys, such as a feather or toy mouse on a string are fabulous for keeping a cat's muscles in tone.

A New Friend

Another possible way to eliminate or reduce stress is to get your cat a companion. Obtaining two cats, particularly kittens or adult cats who know one another and are proven to get along, will not only take some of the burden off of you, but can also help prevent stress as the cats keep one another company and don't need quite as much human interaction.

Clues to Your Cat's Behavior

Physical Stressors and Your Cat

The following is a list of physical triggers that could cause your cat to feel stressed, and thus possibly bring on behavioral problems.

* Breeding
* Illness or injury
* Obesity
* Parasite
* Surgery

Keep in mind, however, that an "only cat" will grow accustomed to life alone and if later on you want to get a new cat, trouble could brew up hard and fast. Cats can become very jealous and an only cat will sometimes resent the introduction of another person (whether it's a baby or an adult) into what the cat sees as his home. Two cats raised together will have one another to keep company, but will still need their human companions to love them and care for them. Don't forget to spend time bonding and getting to know your new cat. Each cat you own should have individual attention every day.

Whatever the reason for your cat's misbehavior, the first step in solving the problem is to discover the cause. Now let's see what you can do about it.

How to Be a Positive Influence on Your Cat

In This Chapter You'll Learn:

* Ways to bond with your cat

* The importance of routine

* How to teach your cat good habits

How does a cat see the world? We could get down on our hands and knees and look up at everything, but that won't quite do it, will it? There's more to the way a cat sees his world than what he sees through his eyes. There is what he feels inside and his instincts. Often, the mistakes we humans make when assessing our cat's behavior is that we see things as a human would and not as a cat would. This is natural, of course. After all, we are only human. But when you have a cat with a behavioral problem you need solved, you have to look beyond human to feline.

So, as a human, how do you do that? Start by learning what your cat's needs are. Basically, all cats have the same needs: food, sleep (about 16 hours' worth), bathroom time, play, scratching, and love. Those are the

Begin bonding with your cat as soon as possible. Although this will not ensure perfect behavior, it will help make problems easier to solve in the future.

basics. Now, the specifics will depend on your cat, because like people, all cats have their own unique nuances, tastes, and personalities. Living closely with a cat (particularly an indoor cat), watching the cat, and paying attention to what you see is the best way to learn what your cat needs, and what would be the preferable approach to solving behavioral problems. Does this sound confusing? It's not, really. Simply put, know your cat.

Bonding with Your Cat

Cat bonding begins at kitten-hood. We already discussed the bond that mother cats create

Earn your cat's trust and his behavioral problems will be easier to solve.

with their kittens and how kittens are influenced by their social contacts and surroundings at different levels dependent upon their age. But once that kitten comes into your life, you must realize that the kitten will still be learning to bond, and how well he bonds will be determined by his past experiences, as well as all future experiences with you. If you want a well-behaved kitty, bonding with your cat at an early age is the first step. Bonding with a cat, in and of itself, is simple. Give your kitty lots and lots of tender loving care, interactive playtimes, and cuddle sessions, and even some of the shyest cats will bond to you with time.

Of course, if merely bonding with your cat would solve all behavioral problems or prevent them from occurring in the first place, this book would not be necessary. Bonding with your cat will do many wondrous things (including giving you a companion and lowering your blood pressure), and one of those things could very well be preventing later problems, but the other great aspect to bonding is that if your cat does develop a nasty habit or problem later on down the line, it will be easier to solve because you will already have the cat's utmost trust and love.

But what if you adopt a cat that already has issues? In this case, bonding might come about more slowly (especially with a shy cat), but in working out your kitty's problems, you will be bonding naturally, as long as your approach is one that is gentle and positive for your cat. So, working out behavioral problems and bonding go hand in hand. One cannot exist without the other successfully. Not easily anyway.

There are many ways to bond with your cat. Try teaching him tricks or even just talking to him.

Your Outta Control Cat

Ways to Bond with Your Cat

* Play with him using catnip and feathers

* Feed him and sit with him while he eats

* Give him treats whenever he does anything good

* Teach your cat tricks

* Watch television with him

* Let him sit on your lap

* Pet your cat while you are on the computer

* Let your cat sleep with you

* Talk to your cat often

* Read to your cat

* Hold him by a window and watch the birds together

The Importance of Routine

Cats are creatures of habit and routine. They get very unsettled if their routine is upset, and many times, this can be the cause of their behavioral problem. A cat that is moved to a new home might start urinating outside the litter box or scratching the kitchen cabinets. A new baby or someone moving in or out of the house will upset a cat's routine. Even the smallest shift can cause a rift in your kitty's habits. To us, this might sound extreme. You certainly can't expect to keep everything exactly the same, never change furniture, don't have a baby, etc. for the cat. However, when you can predict that something is going to happen that will affect the cat (because, let's face it, life throws curve balls all the time that no one can predict), you can take measures to aid your little fur-baby in acclimating to the change. And, as per the unpredictable, there are steps you can take to make it less traumatic.

How to Be a Positive Influence on Your Cat

Keep A Routine

In your cat's everyday life, barring any unusual changes, established routine should be kept firmly in place. For example, the litter box should be in a proper location and not moved around daily or on a whim. Such a feat will send even the most patient cat off to go on the carpet. Some cats like to move their sleeping spot around on their own, but try moving the well-used cat bed and you'll have one disgruntled cat.

Some cats are easy going and accept change more readily than other cats. You might have a cat that can acclimate easily to daily routine changes without a single upset, or you could have a cat that gets upset if you move the sofa to vacuum under it. Get to know your cat, bond with your cat, and you will know how much or how little he can handle and what his boundaries are. Then, perhaps you will know to put him in another room before you move that sofa and pull out the vacuum cleaner.

Teaching Good Habits

The simplest situation for the training of good habits is in the purchase of a new kitten. A young kitten is still impressionable, has not had many life experiences yet, and often hasn't had time to develop bad habits.

Cats are creatures of habit and are most comfortable with a regular routine.

58

The length of time it takes for a cat to adjust to a change in environment is dependent on his personality.

You hold the strings on this unless some strange circumstance has occurred in the kitten's life and caused fear or aggression not usual for a kitten. But even then, retraining will be easier than with an adult cat with a behavioral problem that has gone on long enough to become a bad habit.

Before you even bring your kitten home, you should have a starting point for his routine already set up. In other words, the litter box should be in the location you want it (private, but not so far away the kitten won't want to find it), the scratching post or tree should be available, food and water dishes should be ready, and toys purchased.

The Litter Box

Once kitty is home, make sure he knows where his things are located. Show him the litter box at times when he would be most in need to use

How to Be a Positive Influence on Your Cat

Get your house ready for your new kitten before you bring him home for the first time.

it, such as after eating, after napping, and after play sessions. You can place him in the box and gently hold his paw and rake the litter, but most kittens will get the idea without this step. Once he goes, tell him he's a good kitty and pet him. A cat will be more likely to return to the location of a positive experience than a neutral or negative one. So, if the litter box is a fun place, then the kitten will look forward to using it.

The Scratching Area

Kitten claws are not all that destructive, but they will be, and now is the

Your Outta Control Cat

time to teach the kitten where the appropriate place is to scratch. Never assume that he will know that your sofa is off-limits. He won't. And if your sofa or other furniture is the most convenient place to dig his claws in, that is just what he will do.

Scratching is just as necessary to a cat as going to the bathroom is, and you wouldn't think of having a cat without providing a place for him to do his business, would you? So why get a cat and provide no place for him to sharpen his claws, then act surprised when there are scratches in your sofa?

There are three reasons cats "sharpen" their claws. The first is to sheath off the top layer of claw, leaving a fresh, sharper claw underneath. The second is a territorial purpose. Cats have scent glands located in their paws and when they scratch, they leave their scent for other cats to smell. The third reason they scratch is to stretch the muscles in their back and legs.

Make your kitten's first trip to the litter box a positive experience by praising and petting him after he is finished.

How to Be a Positive Influence on Your Cat

As you can see, "sharpening" is not the only reason cats scratch, and all are important cat-activities. Thus, your kitty should have not only an appropriate area to scratch, but it also should be conveniently located and more attractive than your furniture.

You should introduce your new kitty to the scratching tree the same way you would introduce a litter box. Each day, or even several times per day, show the cat the tree, then gently hold the cat's paws and rake them up and down the post. If you catch the cat with his claws in the wrong place, tell him, "No!" and clap your hands. Then show the cat the right place again. Eventually, if you are persistent, he will get the hint.

These are the guidelines for starting off right with your cat. Even if you acquire an adult cat, the above steps should be followed to some degree. Make sure the cat knows where everything is and doesn't have to search the house to find it.

Your cats should be aware of the location of the litter box and the scratching post so that they don't have to search for those things when they need to use them.

Reward your cat when he does something good. Let him know you love him and you appreciate his good behavior.

Positive Reinforcement

Positive reinforcement simply means that you reinforce good behavior using rewards, rather than punishing the cat when he does something wrong. This is best used during retraining, when the cat already knows what is expected, but something is wrong and he breaks his training. Punishment is unnecessary because the cat already knows that he is not supposed to do that, and he does not need to be reminded. But for some reason known only in the feline mind, the cat is not doing what he is supposed to.

For example, if your recently hospitalized cat comes home after having a urinary disorder, he might

Positive Correction

If the cat eliminates in the wrong place, do not yell at him. Put him in the right place, give him treats, and make the experience a positive one. Then when he does do the right thing, he should be praised for it. That is what positive reinforcement is all about.

How to Be a Positive Influence on Your Cat

Instead of punishing your cat, use positive reinforcement to teach him to continue his good behavior.

associate the litter box with the discomfort he feels and will avoid the box. This is not your kitty doing something wrong. This is your kitty knowing that it simply no longer feels right to do what he is supposed to do. To punish him would only make matters worse, for then he would grow to not trust you, and this can reduce the level of success in training and set things backward rather than progressing forward. So, with the positive reinforcement method of retraining, you always use reward and not punishment.

How to Socialize Your Cat

It's always exciting to bring home a new cat or kitten. Watching the new pet explore his new home, discover the new toys you have laid out for him, and munch on food in his brand new bowls can be very exciting for a new owner. The prospect of acquiring your new kitty is also so exciting that not enough pre-thought might be given to the planning and preparing for the arrival. This should be no less a task than preparing for the arrival of a new baby. You should set up everything your cat will need before you bring him home and prepare the other members of your family (both human and animal) for the new arrival.

Your cat will become a member of your family and it is important that kitty get off to the right start as a member of your household.

Everything will be new and somewhat intimidating to the new cat, so do all you can to make this introductory process stress-free for everyone involved. In time, your new cat will be a welcome, well-adjusted member of your family.

After a period of adjustment, your new cat will become a member of your family.

Making Your Cat Part of the Family

We have already established that cats are creatures of habit, so any new cat you bring into your home is going to have to go through an obvious period of adjustment. Depending on the cat's personality, this could take a bit of time and a period of acclimation. If the cat is shy, this adjustment period may be longer than if the cat is outgoing. Give your shy kitty time and leave him alone for a little while.

Quick Rules for Smooth Introductions

* Make it positive
* Take it slow
* Be patient
* No loud noises or parties
* Utilize caution when introducing other animals
* Give the cat time to adjust

He will find a place to hide where he feels safe and secure, and the only intervention from you (providing the place he chooses is safe for him to be in) should be to place his food, water, and litter box near that location so he does not have to search the house looking for it. Some cats, when new to a situation, will not seek out the litter box but will simply go in a spot close to where they are hidden. This can be the start of behavior problems that will only get worse if they are not nipped in the bud. You can help your cat by following some simple steps. For instance, don't hold any large gatherings or parties for a while after the new cat comes to your home. Too much noise and strange people will more than likely offset any effort on your part to socialize the cat later on, or it may make him permanently afraid, depending on his personality.

Give your kitten time to adjust to his new surroundings. Eventually he will become comfortable with both his environment and his new family.

How to Socialize Your Cat

Each day, several times per day, sit with him and talk softly and soothingly to your cat. Don't try to drag him out of his hiding place or force him to socialize at this point. Keep rambunctious children and all other pets away from him. He will eventually come out on his own, although, depending on the cat, this might take anywhere from a few days to months. At this point there should be only one person (or two at the most), keeping company with him at any given moment. You don't want the cat inundated with too many faces popping in at him. Introductions to other family members and strangers will come later. Let your new cat adjust to you and the new environment first. Eventually, as he adjusts to your presence and emerges from hiding, you can slowly begin the introduction to other people.

If your cat is not all that shy but still seems a bit apprehensive, let him stay in hiding for a day or so. When he wanders out, show him where his food, water, and litter box are. Show him these things several times in the next few days, and don't forget the positive reinforcement. Praise the cat every time he does things correctly.

When holding your cat, keep him close to your body so he feels supported.

Introductions to People

Once your cat has become comfortable in the house, introductions will be in order. First, you want to introduce him to immediate family members, then strangers. If the cat was shy and has only recently come out of hiding, some people living in the house might not have formally met

Your Outta Control Cat

Holding the Cat

Once the cat seems comfortable with the children you have introduced him to, teach the children the proper way to pick up a cat. To do this, you need to know the proper way of picking up a cat yourself. One hand should be underneath and supporting the cat's hind end, while the other should be under the cat's front paws, supporting the front end. The cat should be held close to your body so he feels secure. Never hold a cat out and away from your body.

Of course, every cat is different and once your cat is a member of the family and completely comfortable with you, you might discover a non-traditional way to hold him that he enjoys. For example, my cat Shadow likes to be cradled on his back like a baby.

him yet. Introductions should be slow and gradual, particularly for a shy cat. Your best bet, particularly for cats that are shy, would be to introduce the adults first. Make sure you only introduce one person at a time as to not overwhelm your new cat.

Have the person sit on the floor (more at "cat level" which is less intimidating for the cat), and pet the cat gently. He or she can also feed the cat treats, particularly if the cat does not want to come out of hiding. If the cat seems anxious to get away, let him. Forcing him to stay will only reverse your efforts and frighten the cat more. Keep things low-key and quiet, and make no sudden moves or loud noises. Always be gentle with your new pet, regardless of the cat's personality.

Introducing Cats to Children

If you have young children, it is best to make sure any cat you acquire has an outgoing personality. Children like to play, and this can frighten an already shy cat into further withdrawal. However, even if you have

Children can be wonderful playmates for a cat. Supervise the way they interact, making sure to teach the children to treat the cat with gentle respect.

acquired a cat that is shy, this does not mean that you have to give him up. It does mean that introductions will have to be slower and processed with more caution than introductions with an outgoing cat and adults.

Any child's activity around the cat, particularly in the beginning, should be supervised. Take the child's hand in your own and show him the best and easiest way to stroke the cat without excessive movement or force. Children always mean well but can sometimes hit when they mean to pet. This would not be good, even with an outgoing cat. If your new cat had no previous exposure to children, he might be extremely apprehensive, and the wrong move could make him permanently afraid of children. Be sure to explain to the child that this is a living cat with feelings and is not a toy. Tell the child that he or she needs to be gentle at all times. Never let more than one child crowd the cat, particularly in the beginning.

Some cats will be jealous of a new baby. To prepare your cat for the new arrival, try to introduce him to baby things (such as the sound of a baby crying or the smell of baby powder) before the new child is born.

How to Socialize Your Cat

Cats and Babies

What if you are expecting a baby and your cat has never been around babies? It's amazing to think of the number of people who believe that they must give up their cat because they are expecting a baby. They fear diseases, such as toxoplasmosis, or jealousy from the cat (particularly an existing cat). Jealousy can be avoided or lessened. Some cats may seem jealous when a new baby comes into the home, others might be aloof. If possible, introduce your cat to baby sights, sounds, and smells before the arrival of the infant. Set up a tape recording with the sound of a baby crying, play with your cat around the baby's toys, read baby books to your cat (honest!), or create a "day with baby" by fabricating a day that will be similar to what you will have once the baby arrives. Be sure to give your cat plenty of attention.

Once the baby arrives, introduce the cat slowly. The cat might be frightened of the baby's crying at first, but he will grow accustomed to the sound. In the beginning, keep the cat out of the baby's room and away from the crib unless you are there to supervise. Cats often snuggle where it's warm and this could be in the crib with the baby. Your cat might be trying to show affection to the new child, but the fact is a 12-

Litter Box Concerns

Toxoplasmosis is a disease that can cause birth defects in children and is often the reason women give up their cats when they are expecting a baby. Although it's true that toxoplasmosis can be spread to pregnant women through the feces of a cat, it can easily be avoided with care. If you are pregnant, either get someone else to clean the litter box or wear rubber gloves when you clean the litter box. Always wash your hands thoroughly after handling the litter box.

Your Outta Control Cat

If you have a cat and you're looking to add another to the family, try to find one with a similar personality so they will have a better chance of getting along. Many times two cats will be great playmates even if they were not raised together.

pound cat lying atop a small infant can have dire consequences. Once the child is old enough and big enough to handle the cat's weight, the main caution that should always be taken is to prevent scratches or bites by teaching the child how to behave around and handle a cat.

Introducing Other Cats

Like children, introductions to other cats will have to be done carefully and with much supervision. The difference, however, is that you can't explain to a cat how to behave like you can to a child. Your cat might accept and love the new family member outright (particularly if your kitty is young and so is the other cat), while other cats might become defensive and angry. If you are acquiring a cat as a companion for a resident cat, try to get one with a similar personality, manner, activity level, and age. It has been suggested that the best combination would

How to Socialize Your Cat

When your new cat is introduced to your resident cat, there may be some hissing back and forth. If necessary, separate the cats and try to allow them to get used to the new scents before bringing them back together.

be a male cat with a female but usually after a cat has been fixed it doesn't matter. Many shelters offer spaying and neutering to cats they adopt out.

Introductions to a household are best done when a cat is young. Most people do adopt kittens and this is the simplest acclimation. The following introduction method is recommended:

Place the new cat in a private room, complete with food, water, and litter box and let your resident cats sniff around the door. This should aid the cats in learning each other's scents before they come face to face. Don't be surprised if, despite the door between them, there is some hissing between the cats. If an object (such as a towel or cat bed) came with the newcomer, place this in the region with your resident cats so they can sniff it and also use it as a way to grow accustomed to the new scent.

If you have the resources and room to do this, move your new cat to a different location in the house, then let the resident cats into the room your new cat was in so they may sniff around.

The next step, once the cats appear more comfortable with one another, is to try placing your new cat in a cat carrier with a barred door and then letting the cats smell each other through the door. Again, expect plenty of hissing and growling.

If you have the time, room, and resources, you can keep the new cat in his own room for a couple of days or more, or even switch rooms, and move the cat daily for a few days to various rooms (don't forget to move the litter box, food, and water).

Once you feel ready, let your new cat or kitten mingle with your resident cats. Keep an eye on them, and don't let them run off, particularly if they are still hissing. You can also try feeding them together. If you acquire a kitten and have an older cat, watch them closely. A spunky kitten may pester an older cat relentlessly.

Unfortunately, there may be times when your resident cat will simply not accept a newcomer into the house, particularly an only-cat who

A Positive Association

You can also try feeding your resident cats near the door to where the new cat is being kept. This will give resident cats something positive with which to associate the new cat. Remember, always keep it positive and give resident cats plenty of attention during this time so they will not feel abandoned. Visit the new cat frequently as well for calm reassurance.

A New Friend

An only-cat might be even less patient with the antics of a young kitten than cats in a multi-cat family are. Keeping the kitten busy with toys and games or acquiring two kittens might help take the pressure off the older cat. However, in some cases, a kitten will actually bring out the friskiness in an older cat.

How to Socialize Your Cat

Allow your new cat to mingle with the resident cats, keeping a close eye on them to make sure they are getting along.

has been alone for quite some time. Give it time. Don't assume that because your cats are still hissing at the sight of one another after only three days that they will never get along. Sometimes it can take weeks or even months. Usually two to four weeks is the recommended amount of time to give two cats to learn to accept one another. If all else fails, ask your veterinarian to recommend a good cat therapist.

Introducing Your Cat To Dogs

You have heard the cliché "fighting like cats and dogs" many times. This cliché does not have to be a reality if cats and dogs are raised together or are introduced properly. Some cats and dogs seem to be natural friends, and others natural enemies. I have known cats that lay on the floor with dogs, lick their faces, and knead them, while other cats cannot stand the sight of a dog even through a window. Introducing new cats to other animals, particularly dogs, requires more caution than when introducing a cat to another cat. If you are introducing your new cat to a dog that has never been around cats before, introductions will require utmost care and patience.

Regardless of whether you think the dog will be fine with the cat, always introduce the cat at the dog's eye level, and hold both carefully. If the dog seems agitated or aggressive, remove the cat and

try again at another time. Never leave the cat and dog together unsupervised until they are perfectly comfortable and accustomed to one another, and you know beyond a doubt that there will not be any sneak attacks while you are away.

If your resident cat does not accept a new cat into the family, give it some time. If more than a month has passed, consider taking your feline to a cat therapist.

How to Socialize Your Cat

Let the cat and dog get to know and become comfortable with one another before leaving them alone together.

Usually cats that have grown up with a dog or a puppy will be more accustomed to dogs in general, and it will be easier to introduce that cat to a new dog. If you acquire a puppy, things should go a bit smoother with introductions. A puppy, like a kitten, has not yet fully developed the instincts it will have as an adult, and the most trouble you will probably run into will be the puppy's unending energy. A puppy will see your cat as another puppy to play with. Though a cat is intelligent enough and able to defend himself if the puppy becomes too rowdy, a declawed cat, an ill cat, or a more sedentary cat may not be able to defend himself or get away from the puppy's advances. Be careful the puppy (particularly a large breed) does not hurt the cat with his enthusiasm to play or wear an older cat out by not letting him have any peace.

Introducing Cats to Other Animals

Certain other pets might not need formal introductions to your cat, particularly pets such as reptiles and other caged animals, if there is no chance your cat will have contact with these pets. However, if your cat will be interacting with these animals on a regular basis, you will need to introduce them. Even after introductions, never leave a cat alone with these types of pets. Make sure the cages they are kept in are secure with tight lids. A cat's natural instinct is to play with or even kill these animals, depending on the cat's background and personality.

Some cats will never be able to interact with "prey" animals safely. Others will mother these pets and treat them as if they were the cat's own babies. To introduce a rodent, bird, or reptile to your new cat, hold the pet carefully and watch the cat's response. If his instinct seems to be to attack, take the animal away. Otherwise, let them interact and keep a close watch.

If possible, introduce your pets while they are still young so that when they are older they will be good friends.

How to Socialize Your Cat

Cats and Ferrets

Ferrets are a bit different. Many people think cats would view them as prey, but generally cats and ferrets get along well. It is usually the ferret, with its playful and rambunctious nature, that intimidates the cat in most cases. Ferrets have extremely tough skin and can play very rough, and don't understand that the cat's skin isn't as rugged as their own. Make sure the cat is not frightened of the ferret and that the ferret is comfortable around the cat. Generally, more active cats will get along best with ferrets. However, as with any other animal, supervise play activities carefully until the animals are accustomed to one another and you are positive no harm will come to either pet.

If your cat needs to be reintroduced to a member of your household, animal or human, take it slowly and be patient.

Reintroductions

If you need to reintroduce a person or an animal to your cat, the procedure should be almost the same as with the first introduction, with slight moderations depending upon why the reintroduction needs to occur. If the family dog scared your cat, those introductions will need to be remade very slowly and carefully. The two pets should not be left alone together until there is no chance that harassment of any kind will occur.

If your cat came to you with a fear of someone in particular or perhaps a fear of children, you

Your Outta Control Cat

Contrary to popular belief, cats are quite capable of following house rules. Be patient and consistent with your cat, rewarding him when he is good and punishing him when he misbehaves.

How to Socialize Your Cat

will have to reintroduce children very slowly. In a case such as this, you will want to acclimate the cat to children using the methods described previously. Introduce different children, one at a time, and let the cat get used to one child before introducing another.

Basically, keep the cat's needs in mind whether introducing a person for the first time or reintroducing someone. Remember, cats cannot understand your words when you tell them this is okay and they should relax. You have to show them. You have to think on the cat's level. Doing this will bring you closer to your cat and allow for a stronger bond and better introductions.

Introducing Your Cat to House Rules

You can introduce your cat to people and other animals easily enough, but you also need to introduce him to rules of the house in order to prevent having a monster cat on your hands. Many people believe that

If your cat insists on lounging on a certain piece of furniture, try using a water bottle or "scat mat" to deter him.

Rules of Play

Often, play is viewed as aggression to a person. Sometimes when two cats play it appears that they are fighting, or when a cat suddenly leaps out and attacks you it might appear that the cat is being aggressive. This is either play or the cat relaying you a message.

For example, your cat might attack your hand suddenly if he no longer feels like being handled. Any behaviors you do not like and want halted must be worked at. A quick squirt of water (if you know when the cat will "attack") or a shake at the scruff of the neck can give your cat the message you are upset.

cats are incapable of learning rules due to their seemingly aloof nature and tendency to want things done their way, but this is not the truth. Cats are intelligent animals and quite capable of learning rules and even tricks when taught properly and with patience.

Always utilize persistence, patience, and consistency when teaching rules to a cat. It is important to remember that any rule (such as not jumping on tables) you want your kitten to adhere to in adulthood must be taught right from the beginning. Try not to lapse in keeping rules just because the kitten is cute or the cat is new to the house, only to punish the cat later when the novelty of ownership has worn off. You'll want your cat to know as soon as possible the rules you've established. A cat does not understand why he was allowed on the table or counter as a kitten and is punished for the same behavior as an adult cat.

A water squirt bottle is a good device to deter cats. Keep it near the area where you do not want the cat to go and make sure to use it if the cat misbehaves. Don't ever yell at or hit your cat. You don't want the cat to be afraid of you just to learn that this is the wrong behavior. Of

How to Socialize Your Cat

If you do not enjoy finding your cats lounging on your bed, a scat mat can be useful in breaking this habit.

course, some cats only do the wrong behavior when the owner is not around. If you worry that this will happen with your cat, then you might want to try keeping him confined while no one is there to supervise him. Confinement should not be for long periods of time and should only be a temporary situation while training.

You can also trying getting "scat mats." These can be found in pet supply stores and catalogues. These mats are placed on the counter, table, sofa, or anywhere you want the cat to avoid. They give off a very slight electric shock when touched. (The shock doesn't hurt the cat and is equivalent to that of static electricity.) These generally work better than a squirt bottle because there is no association to you on the cat's part, and you don't have to confine the cat when you are not home.

Your Outta Control Cat

This pad can also be used if you wish to keep your cat off your bed if you do not keep the door closed. Some people have allergies and need to keep the cat away from their sleeping area, or they may have a particularly rambunctious cat that loves to chase toes in the middle of the night. Whatever the reason, simply keeping the door closed does not always work unless the cat has been well trained from kittenhood to stay out and not try to bang the door down when it is closed.

As with any other rule, teaching the cat to stay out of a room is a task that requires patience and persistence. A cat that has always been allowed in the bedroom and suddenly isn't anymore will probably not accept this change lightly. The cat wants to be with you and does not understand why he suddenly can't. He may wail and cry outside the door, scratch, and try to stick his paws under the door, (as if he can lift the door up enough to slip under). You can try keeping the cat in another room, but chances are his wailing will keep you awake anyway.

With patience and proper training, your cat can be taught to behave the way you want him to.

If your cat is not allowed to sleep in your bedroom, set up a special place just for him where he will be comfortable and content.

A Place to Cat Nap

If you do not want your cat sleeping with you in your bedroom, you can give your cat a bed all his own. Try setting up a special place with his own special bed in a location you and your cat would both like, (such as by a window where it is nice and sunny). Sprinkling catnip on the bed you choose for your cat and playing with the cat in it will help the cat create a pleasant association with the bed.

Most pet stores and pet supply catalogues sell cat beds and there is usually a vendor at every cat show that sells them. Cat beds range from pads you can place anywhere you wish to wicker baskets or elaborately decorated and colored cat "palaces." Whichever bed you choose, it should be soft, comfortable, and washable. Some beds have cedar mattresses to repel fleas. However, this is not recommended as cedar can cause respiratory problems in some cats.

Your Outta Control Cat

Keep your cat's bed clean and dry because cats are meticulously clean and most are opposed to sleeping in soiled areas. This includes cleaning the frame of the bed as well as the pad. Beds with removable pads, which can be thrown in the washing machine are available, or you can place a towel inside the bed. Some beds are washable by themselves.

Training Your Cat to Sleep in a Crate

Training an animal to sleep in a cage (or crate, as they are often referred to) is generally an activity associated with dogs, but cats can be "trained" to use a crate, depending upon the circumstances involved. Usually a cage is best restricted to kittens, but stores sell large "cat playpens" that some cats find comfortable. Training a cat to accept a cage is best done during kittenhood when the kitten is most trainable. Some cats, such as show cats, learn to love and accept sleeping in cages. As long as the cat is not kept in a cage continuously and the cage is only used when necessary, this should not be a problem.

A Separate Litter Box

Having another litter box and practicing confinement either through the use of a crate or in a room can come in handy when a new cat or kitten has special needs.

Not long ago, an older cat fell into my mother's hands. The cat had many health problems and needed to be kept separated from the other cats. Some of the cat's health issues included medicines that can cause a cat the need to urinate frequently. Since the cat had to be kept away from the other cats, a litter box and separate accommodations were provided in another room. This was a natural method of training the previously outdoor cat the art of sticking to the litter box and it is a lesson he never forgot.

Keep your cat's napping sites clean and dry.

A crate can be either an all-wire cage or a large airline-approved carrier (such as the Nylabone® Fold-Away Pet Carrier). The crate should be large enough so the kitten or cat can play inside, and the cage should also fit a small litter pan, food and water dishes, and the pet's bed. The largest size dog crate often works best because you can hang toys from the bars and there is plenty of room to move around.

We'll discuss crate-training kittens here since most of the time kittens are easier to train to a crate. Adult cats kept in cages should only be kept in tall cat playpens particularly made for adult cats, or else the crate might be too small. However, if a cat is ill, a crate can be used temporarily until the cat is better.

Why would you want to crate train your kitten? For situations when you are not at home or if you want a good night's sleep, crate training is a good idea. Kittens want to play at all hours and frequently get into mischief. Crate training will give you peace of mind and prevent the kitten from harming itself when you are not there to supervise. Crate training also teaches a kitten to eventually accept cat carriers.

Kittens do not resent being confined and will generally sleep in their crate even when it is left open. Line the crate with a clean, dry towel or

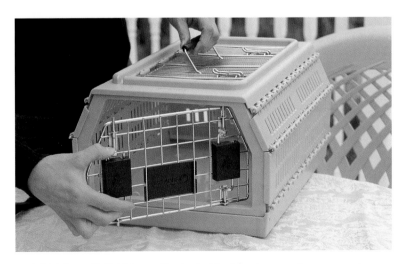

A Nylabone® Fold Away Carrier is ideal for transporting your cat safely.

How to Socialize Your Cat

For the times when you are forced to leave your kitten alone, crate training can come in handy.

blanket. Place the crate in a draft-free area away from people and loud noises.

Keep the cage door open on the first day and show the kitten where the cage is. Make sure he sees his food and water. Place the kitten in the cage and use toys to make the experience a positive one. Speak softly and soothingly to the kitten. Try closing the door, but if the kitten panics, open it again. You do not want any negative associations with the crate, which will eventually become your cat's own special place.

If the kitten seems reasonably content, walk away for a few minutes, then return and open the door. Continue this throughout the day, leaving the kitten for longer and longer periods of time. Place your kitten in the crate after playtime and when he is tired. Walk away and leave the kitten alone. Make no fuss, even if he cries, and soon your precious little bundle of fur will be sound asleep. Make sure that your kitten has plenty of playtime and family interaction outside the crate more times than not.

Through positive reinforcement and with patience, your new cat can learn to socialize and interact with other pets and family members. Your cat is a member of your family and it is important that everyone in the household get along.

Practical Solutions to Pesky Problems

In This Chapter You'll Learn:

✳ Reasons why your cat may stop using the litter box

✳ How to train and retrain your cat when necessary

✳ How to stop your cat from chewing

✳ How to stop bad biting behaviors

✳ How to deal with mischief-makers

There is no such thing as acquiring a trouble-free pet. Every pet requires care and will come with a set of challenges that you will need to deal with. With fish, it is keeping the water at the correct temperature. With reptiles, it is keeping them warm and in the right environment. But many people think that cats are different. Some people believe that cats are so aloof and so independent that they need almost no care, and that they can be left alone in a small apartment and will just sleep the whole time. However, this type of thinking often leads to behavioral problems. Caring for a cat requires more energy and effort than just providing food and water and giving the cat a pat on the head once in awhile. No cat is perfect, and each one will come with his or her own set of quirks and idiosyncrasies. This chapter will help you cope with the some of the pesky problems associated with owning a cat.

Once you cat has been trained to use his litter box, there still may be occasions where he refuses to use it. This behavior can be influenced by a variety of factors.

Indiscriminate Urination

The number one reason cats are turned over to shelters is due to indiscriminate urination. This is generally a sign of stress rather than the cat simply being "bad." There can be many causes for this behavior and many people simply give up trying to fix the problem. If you truly love your cat and giving him up isn't an option, then hope is not lost.

Some indiscriminate urination behaviors have already been discussed, such as when a cat is jealous or upset about something, but if your cat is simply refusing to use his litter box, then the box itself might be the culprit.

The Litter Box

What type of litter box do you use? Is it new or has the cat suddenly stopped using the box he always used before? If the box is new, particularly if it is a new design, your cat might need time to get used to the new box, or you might have to go back to the old style.

Some cats don't like covered litter boxes, though most just need to get used to them. Since cats like privacy and most don't mind small spaces, covered boxes are not usually a problem. A box with sides that are too tall for a small cat or kitten could pose a problem. In such a case, get a box with lower sides.

Give your new cat some time to get used to his litter box.

Self-cleaning litter boxes are becoming more popular these days, but some cats are afraid to use them. If you want to use this type of litter box, introduce your cat to it gradually using positive reinforcement and treats to make the experience a happy one. Be sure the cat is out of the box when the self-cleaning mechanism kicks in. Never use these boxes with kittens.

Pick a Good Litter

What kind of litter do you use? At one time, it was common to use sand in a cat's litter box. The belief was that since cats naturally go outside, sand is the most natural substance to use. This may be true, but plain sand may house worms or parasites dangerous to your cat and sand is not very efficient at eliminating odor. With so many litters to choose from on the market today, there is bound to be one that is convenient to you as well as agreeable to your cat.

Practical Solutions to Pesky Problems

Cats are extremely clean animals and will appreciate a dry, fresh-smelling litter box.

Using a commercial box is best because some cats are picky about the material their litter box is made out of. A wooden or cardboard box not only might smell funny to your cat, but such porous material will soak up urine and eventually cause odor problems.

Litter box cleanliness and dryness is a major factor for many cats as they are fastidious creatures that like their potty area to be clean. A clean litter box is also important for your cat's health and well-being. Scooping regularly is important, as is cleaning the box thoroughly when odors start to cling to the box. A box that emanates odors will be unattractive to your cat, as will a box that reeks of strong chemicals, so take care in what you use to clean the box. You can bleach a litter box that is in desperate need of cleaning, but be sure there is no residual bleach smell left behind or your cat might reject the box. Placing the bleached and rinsed box in the sun until it dries is a good idea and will result in a fresh smelling litter box that is attractive to you and your cat.

Make sure the litter in the box stays dry. Moisture breeds germs that cause odors and disease. If you use a scoopable litter, make sure you get all the chunks at the bottom of the box as well as on those on top. Any wet litter should be removed and replaced with dry litter every day.

Location, Location, Location

The location of the litter box and the number of litter boxes per cat is also very important. If the box is too far away, your cat might not want to seek it out and may go wherever it is convenient. At the same time, cats like their privacy, so don't put the box in high traffic areas. Most people choose a corner of the bathroom or a spare bedroom for the litter box. Never place the litter box too close to where your cat eats. Cats don't like to "go" in the same vicinity as their food.

If you absolutely hate the look of the litter box but want to be sure it remains in a location convenient for your cat, you can buy a specialized

Place the litter box in an out-of-the-way location, such as the corner of the bathroom.

Practical Solutions to Pesky Problems

cabinet that houses the litter box in an attractive way. Many pet supply stores or catalogues now offer attractive cabinets (some are even carpeted so your cat will sleep on top of the cabinet) that house litter boxes. Any top-opening chest that sits on the floor can be converted into a litter box cabinet simply by cutting an appropriate sized hole on the side.

Other Litter Box Problems

More serious reasons why your cat might stop using the litter box include territorial difficulties, illness, surgery, or a new location.

Territory

We have discussed territorial instincts previously, and this is the most common problem associated with indiscriminate urination. Cats' instincts for

A cat's hesitation to use his litter box might be a cry for help.

A cat that urinates on the carpet or wall may be unhappy with his litter box.

territory run very strong and marking with urine is one very powerful way of showing who is boss of that area. If your cat is whole (meaning not spayed or neutered), the scent of another cat can cause the territorial instincts to kick in. A male cat may start to spray urine as early as six or seven months if he's not neutered. There may or may not be a female cat present for this to happen. A female cat in heat might also feel a need to mark her territory, and relieve herself in unusual locations. In this case, the obvious solution is to get your cat fixed, preferably by six months of age.

How Much Litter?

It might seem trivial, but the amount of litter you place in the box can make a difference to your cat. If it is too deep, your cat might feel uncomfortable sinking his paws into it. Too little litter won't be much fun to dig in. About an inch or so is usually a comfortable level for most cats.

Practical Solutions to Pesky Problems

Blame the Litter Box

Is your litter box the reason your cat is choosing your carpet to do his business? Some cats are very sensitive to the type of litter box they will use. When choosing a litter box, think of your cat and ask yourself the following questions:

* Is my cat small, and are the sides of the box too high?
* Are the sides too low and my cat keeps hanging off the edge?
* Is the box too big and my cat is getting lost in there?
* Is the box automatic and the mechanism scares my cat?
* Is the litter inside the box too deep or too shallow?
* Is the box in a convenient yet not too crowded location?

A cat that has been fixed might still retain strong territorial instincts, particularly if the cat was fixed at a later age. The scent of another cat, whether a new cat in the house or a cat that is outside, might cause some housecats to feel a need to mark territory. This also leads to competition. If a cat feels that it must compete for food, owner attention, or even the litter box, going in an unacceptable location might be a cry for help.

Illness

Illness can also cause a cat to temporarily or even permanently avoid the litter box. If a cat has been ill, particularly with a urinary disorder (which usually causes urination to be painful), sometimes he will associate his discomfort with the litter box and avoid it. In a case such as this, you will have to retrain him using positive reinforcement, which basically means teaching the cat to accept the litter box once more by replacing the negative association with a positive one.

Surgery

Surgery for declawing (also known as onychectomy, where the claws as well as the last three toe bones are removed) is a very painful operation and the cat's feet are extremely sore and sensitive afterward. Many cats absolutely refuse to use a litter box after this surgery. The gravelly litter is too rough, and they associate the box with their discomfort and ultimately stop using it. This is a hard situation to resolve, as the paws must heal completely before the cat can be reintroduced to the box. Sometimes, with certain sensitive cats, it might be too late by the time the cat's feet heal. Usually, very strict measures can be taken to resolve this problem.

Moving the Box

If you have just moved and your cat has stopped using the litter box, several causes might be considered. If other cats lived in the house previously, and the house was not thoroughly remodeled and sterilized, your cat's sensitive nose might be picking up the other cat's scents. If no other cats lived there, other causes can be suspected. For example,

After an illness, a cat might avoid the litter box. In this case, he will need to be patiently retrained.

Practical Solutions to Pesky Problems

your cat might be unfamiliar with the layout of the house and the litter box is now located in a different place than in the old house. This can cause temporary confusion. Some cats are simply picky, and might not like that you moved them from their comfort zone to this new location.

Disabled cats might have or develop litter box difficulties. For instance, my cat Gillie had to have a hind leg removed because of

To make sure your cat feels comfortable after moving to a new home, help him adjust to the new locations of his belongings, including his litter box.

Your Outta Control Cat

As your cat gets older, be aware of the fact that he might have more trouble getting to the litter box.

cancer. While adjusting to his new situation (which cats do surprisingly well) I gave him a low-sided litter box which was easy to climb in an out of until he had learned to get around easily on three legs and could hop in and out of a regular box.

A blind cat might also have difficulties, so always keep that in mind and make sure that the box is conveniently located, the cat knows where it is, the litter box is kept clean at all times, and it is of the appropriate size for the cat's disability.

Retraining—The Litter Box

The number one reason cats are turned over to shelters is for breaking litter box habits. Often, a cat will suddenly start avoiding the litter box because something negative has happened that has made the cat afraid, or because he made association with the box and an unpleasant

Practical Solutions to Pesky Problems

When a cat starts avoiding the litter box, try to figure out what caused the change in his behavior, and then begin to retrain him.

experience. If this has happened, a whole new set-up may be required.

First, you will have to get rid of whatever caused the cat to avoid the litter box in the first place. If it was due to an illness, then it will only be a matter of re-associating the box in a positive way. If the cat was declawed and associates the box with painful feet, other criteria will have to be set in place first.

How to Retrain Your Cat to Use the Litter Box

The first step is to give the cat a reason to want to use the litter box again. You will have to keep him away from or remove any trace of the preferred location. In other words, clean the area where he has been going and disinfect it well. A cat's nose is very sensitive, so use powerful detergents meant to be used near cats. Anything else could be dangerous if kitty steps in it and licks his paws. Also, be careful not to mix chemicals.

Next, you'll have to make that area unattractive so the cat does not have the desire to go back there. You could put a piece of furniture there, or buy a pad from the pet store that emits a light shock (like a static electricity shock) when the cat steps on it. Some people have even put down tinfoil or double-stick tape to keep kitty away from that area. You could also place the food and water on the location, on top of a mat. Cats don't like to eliminate near where they eat, although an old

Your Outta Control Cat

Before you begin retraining your cat to use the litter box, keep him from returning to the area where he has been going by cleaning and disinfecting it well.

Practical Solutions to Pesky Problems

Keep It Clean

Cleanliness is very important to cats. Always keep the litter box clean and dry and remember to scoop it regularly. Also, when your cat has an accident outside of the litter box, be sure to clean and disinfect the area thoroughly.

or sick cat might not care as much and only be looking for a location that is convenient. If this is the case, you should rethink your setup and change for the cat.

Place a litter box (filled with litter the cat likes) near the location where the cat has been going. If he has been going in more than one area, make all areas unattractive and place the litter box near the area he uses the most. This is only temporary.

Show your kitty where the box is and put him in it, praising him and giving him treats to show him that this is where he is supposed to go and that this is a good place. You can even gently dig his feet in the box for him, to show him what is expected of him. If he uses the box, make a fuss, and tell him what a good kitty he is. If he hops out and walks away, fine. Let him. Once he is going in this box, you can slowly start to move it to where you want it. But this has to be a gradual process. Move the box a small amount of space each day or every other day, making sure that your kitty still sees it and is

When retraining your cat to use the litter box, talk to him and make him feel comfortable so he begins to associate the litter box with positive, pleasant feelings.

still using it, until the box is back where you want it.

If it is completely inconvenient to do this, then make the area where he has been going as unattractive as possible so he avoids it, and show him where the new litter box is as often as possible. You might also want to try changing the box and using a new litter, so the cat does not associate the box with the same negative experience as before.

Having a clean litter box is very important to your cat.

Confine the Cat

Keep up this training daily and don't let it slip or you could have problems. Remember how important routine is for a cat. Show the box to him during the day. If you cannot be home, confine him to another room if possible, with a new litter box, food, and water. A small room will be preferable, particularly if it is a room where he will have little opportunity to go on the floor or anywhere but in the box. This will help reinforce the training and once he has learned where he is supposed to go and is going there regularly, you can stop confining him.

Another method is a complete confinement method, which might work for you if you can't be moving litter boxes around all the time but have room to confine the cat for extended periods. While you are there to supervise, let your kitty go about his daily business, but if you are not there, confine him. Also, confine him when you feed him and wait for him to use the litter box. Praise him when he uses the box and then release

Practical Solutions to Pesky Problems

When retraining a cat, follow the same rules you would for a kitten, including confining him to the litter box after waking and eating.

him. Do the same after he wakes, eats, or plays, just as you would with a kitten, and eventually your cat will learn to associate the box with these activities and with praise.

Sometimes a combination of the above methods works. If your cat is an outdoor cat that needs to be brought in and looks at the litter box as if it was a monster, then the confinement method will not only teach your cat litter box etiquette, but also help acclimate him to indoor life.

Training and Retraining—Scratching

All cats, save the cheetah, have retractable claws. What this means is that there is a sheath within the paw that the claw retracts into. Claws are extensions of your cat's skin, and a complex union of the epidermal structure is attached to the terminal bones of the toe.

Provide a place for your cats to scratch so that they don't choose the furniture for a scratching post.

Practical Solutions to Pesky Problems

You may need to provide your cat with more than one place to scratch, especially if you have multiple cats.

As discussed earlier, cats have a definite need to scratch. If you do not provide a proper place for your cat to satisfy this most natural of behaviors, he will find his own place to do it, and that place might not be where you had in mind. If your cat scratches where he shouldn't, don't blame the cat. What you need to do is teach your cat where the appropriate location is to scratch as well as where the inappropriate locations are. Redirect his instincts to the right place. To do this, you have to provide the cat with the appropriate place to scratch. If you don't, and the cat claws your sofa, you have only yourself to blame.

Scratching Tools

So, where is this appropriate place? Well, it is not only a where, but a what. Cat trees and scratching posts are available at almost any pet supply location and come in a variety of colors, sizes, shapes, and materials. You need to purchase one that your cat will use and enjoy more than your furniture. Buying a small post for a big cat that will just tip it over every time he scratches will be useless. Your sofa will be much more fun.

Sometimes you might need more than one cat tree or post, or a combination of them, depending on how many cats you have and how

Room at the Top

A cat tree with multiple tiers will also give your cats a place to sleep. Cats like high vantage points, so the higher the better. If you can, purchase cat trees with enough tiers for each cat in the house (three cats should have a three-tiered tree), though some cats might still squabble over a certain tier, particularly the one on the top.

much scratching they do. All cats have their preference of materials they like to scratch (some prefer wood, others carpet, still others love sisal rope, and so on), so for this reason, particularly in a multi-cat household, the best tree you can purchase is a large multi-tiered, multi-material tree. Having more than one tree is preferable if you have multiple cats or if your single kitty likes to scratch in many different locations. The more attractive and convenient the appropriate scratching area, the less attractive the inappropriate area will become, and this is your key to saving furniture.

Placement of the scratching post or tree is also key. Where does your cat like to scratch? Some cats like to claw the wood on the edging of walls or doorways, while others prefer

If you have more than one cat, a cat tree may be a good purchase. Each cat can have their own tier and high vantage point.

Practical Solutions to Pesky Problems

the sofa or a chair. Some cats like to scratch the carpeting. This will not only affect the decision on which materials the tree should be made of, but it will also affect placement within the house. You want to place the tree in a location where your cat is going to use it. Cats love window views. They like to watch the trees and birds and often their favorite scratching location is the living room, where there usually is a good window for bird watching.

Give your cat plenty of opportunity to scratch in the right place by offering a variety of appropriate scratching surfaces. In addition to your average cat trees and posts, there are many varieties of smaller scratch pads that might be useful to your kitty when he is in a room away from the tree. These are usually not good to use as the only scratching surface because they rarely provide for all of kitty's needs. These are usually made of corrugated cardboard, which can be fun to scratch, but often it moves or is not steady enough

Once the blinds are opened, this cat will be in heaven. Cats love to look out the window and observe the birds.

Your Outta Control Cat

The Right Cat Tree

The cat tree you choose should be one your cat will love, not one you found convenient because it was small and low-priced. Most small posts are useless with most cats, as they cannot get a good stretch. Often, these posts will be ignored and your sofa will take the brunt of kitty's needs. The following is a guide for choosing the right tree or post for your cat.

Kittens generally don't need to scratch and their claws do little damage until they reach adolescence. Starting out with a regular-sized carpeted post will be sufficient until kitty gets bigger (unless you have an unusually large kitten who likes to stretch to full length, then you will need something taller). Always remember that no matter what tree or post you purchase, the base should always be the widest area to prevent tipping. Adult cats should have cat trees, as opposed to posts. These trees should be multi-tiered, preferably made of various materials (carpet, wood, sisal rope) with a wide base to prevent tipping.

for most cats. But they can, however, provide entertainment, particularly if treated with catnip (for a cat that responds well to catnip, not all cats do).

What about the decision of providing one cat tree or two, or a variety? It will depend on your cat and how many cats reside in the house. If you place a small post in the main room where your cat adores clawing up the sofa and chairs, then that behavior will probably continue, because, let's face it, that sofa is bigger and more fun than that little post! The trick is in making the cat tree or appropriate scratching area the most alluring location for this instinct. The more cat trees and/or posts you provide, the more likely your cat will be to scratch these areas and leave your furniture alone.

Practical Solutions to Pesky Problems

Training Your Cat to Use the Scratching Posts

Next you have to train your cat to use these posts and trees. Usually, if you buy a cat tree that is tall and attractive enough for your cat, you will need to do very little if anything to teach your cat to use it. When a new cat comes into your life and your home, you will simply have to show him where the cat tree is. Teach him from the start where he can scratch and where he cannot.

Reinforce the training by frequently showing the cat the tree. Make sure that the tree is in the location the cat frequents the most or he might be reluctant to use it if he has to seek it out.

In retraining, you might want to keep a squirt bottle handy near the inappropriate area the cat is likely to scratch. Since most cats despise being squirted by water, this is a good deterrent. However, it does nothing to teach a cat who scratches when you are not home to catch him. For

If you show your cat where the scratching post is, it may be all the training he needs in this area.

this reason, confinement during training or retraining might be necessary. If you need to confine your cat temporarily while you are not home to supervise, make sure he has plenty of food and water, a window view, litter box, and the cat post/tree. It would also help if there were no temptations for scratching the wrong area. If you place the cat in a room with lots of furniture he likes, the bad behavior will be reinforced and the good behavior will be discouraged.

While one multi-tiered tree can accommodate several cats, the more trees and posts you have, the more likely it is that your cat will leave the furniture alone.

Practical Solutions to Pesky Problems

Quick Solutions

A few temporary but successful methods in diverting cats away from furniture include: shock pads that can be bought at pet supply stores (they emit a light static electricity shock when the cat steps on them), balloons placed in the area the cat likes to scratch most (if a balloon pops whenever the kitty tries to scratch the wrong area, he will eventually fear that area. Don't use this with unusually shy or fearful cats, however), double-stick tape placed over the most-scratched area, tinfoil (or any other substance cats hate putting their claws on), plastic sofa covers, and keeping the cat tree or post right next to the area the cat likes best.

To encourage your cat's use of the appropriate area, play with him near and on the scratching tree, give him treats, and rub catnip into the fibers of the tree. Make this area as attractive to your cat as you can. This is the key and can't be stressed strongly enough. If you draw your kitty to

Use treats or toys to lure your cat off of the furniture and attract him to the scratching tree.

To discourage cats from climbing on the furniture, try placing shock pads or inflated balloons on the areas you want them to stay away from.

the right place and discourage him from the wrong place, he will learn to use the tree.

Keep patience and persistence in mind at all times, and make sure everyone in the house is consistent in helping with your cat's training. Soon you will have a well-trained cat and no worries about finding your furniture shredded.

Chew On This

Your new kitten has been chewing on your favorite blanket or your hand. Why? Chewing can be either natural in origin or can be caused by something else, such as a medical problem or a behavioral problem. Is your kitten about four months of age or a bit older? Perhaps she is cutting new teeth. Just like babies and puppies, kittens chew because it soothes the gums during teething. In a case like this, your cat is just being a cat.

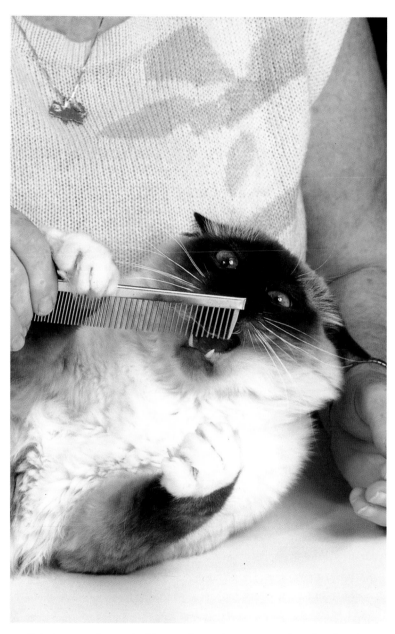

Cats love to play and will sometimes chew on your hand or feet (or other objects) during a game. To keep this from happening, immediately take hold of your cat and sternly say, "No" so he understands that biting is unacceptable.

Your Outta Control Cat

Play Biting

Sometimes your cat or kitten will bite you during play. Play biting can start in kittenhood and become a real problem once the cat becomes an adult. If your kitten seems to get a kick out of chewing on your hand or attacking your feet, don't worry; this is a form of play. However, if you do not want an adult cat with sharp teeth gnawing on your hand later on, teach the cat to stop this behavior immediately. Grab the cat and firmly tell him, "No." Make sure the he understands that this is not acceptable behavior, and remember to be consistent with your correction. Lack of consistency only instills confusion, which can make the behavior worse.

Fur-Biting

Perhaps you have started noticing that your cat is developing bald patches in his fur. He has been chewing on himself and you do not know why. If this is the case, your first priority is to check him for fleas. Look through the cat's fur and check for tiny specks that look like pepper. If you see any, chances are that your cat has fleas. Depending on how severe the case of fleas is, you might want to take your cat to the veterinarian for professional treatment. If there are no parasites, another physical malady might be the reason for

If your cat is suddenly interested in chewing on everything, he may be teething.

Practical Solutions to Pesky Problems

Poisonous Plants

The following is a list of some of the plants that can be poisonous or at the least make your cat sick if he eats them. If you have any of these plants (and this list is not complete, so find out if you are unsure), keep them well out of your cat's reach.

Arrowhead vine	Jasmine
Caladium	Laurel
Christmas berries	Mistletoe
Chrysanthemum	Nutmeg
Creeping Charlie	Philodendron
Daffodil	Poinsettia
Dieffenbachia	Poppy
Holly	Mums
Ivy (all kinds)	

the fur-biting. Explain the situation to the vet and have the vet give your cat a complete physical. If your cat receives a clean bill of health, then there might be a psychological reason behind the fur-biting. Has anything changed in your cat's environment? If so, follow the procedure that was addressed in previous chapters.

Sometimes the presence of another cat can cause a cat to become frustrated and literally "tear his hair out." Overgrooming is often a sign of stress, and stress is caused by changes, either major or minor, to the cat's environment. Your veterinarian might want to suggest a spray or ointment that will keep your cat from chewing on himself while you work on finding the cause of the stress and eliminating it.

Chewing on Plants

Some cats love to chew on plants. This is normal, as cats often crave roughage and if they are outside, they will eat grass. Although this can

Many cats enjoy chewing on plants and the greenery can aid in digestion, but be sure to carefully observe the plants your pet nibbles on.

While cats can often find a way to reach whatever it is they want to get, keeping plants out of reach is a good way to ensure that he won't eat any greenery that could be harmful to him.

help aid in their digestion, you want to be careful. Some plants can make your cat ill, and others are downright deadly.

To keep your cat from chewing your houseplants, provide him with his own garden. This is particularly important for indoor cats that can't chew on grass outside. You can provide your cat with freshly grown catnip and cat greens, all of which are easy to grow and can be bought at pet stores in convenient kits complete with instructions on how to grow and tend them.

Growing these is no guarantee, however, that your cat will not touch your plants if they are within the cat's reach. There are several solutions to this problem. You can keep your plants out of the cat's reach (which can sometimes be difficult because cats are avid climbers and jumpers), buy a non-toxic spray that is made especially to keep your cat away from the houseplants, or enclose your plants behind a screen or glass.

Your Outta Control Cat

If your cat develops a habit of chewing on just about anything, try to find the cause of this change in behavior.

Practical Solutions to Pesky Problems

Cats love to play. Spending time with your feline friend will help him to feel loved and keep him out of trouble.

Chewing on Blankets and Clothes

What if you give your cat plenty of greens to munch on, but he is still chewing on your blankets and/or clothes? Believe it or not, some cats do develop strange chewing habits. Wool and plastic seem to be among the favorites for cats who like to chew. The reason for this behavior can be varied. Sometimes a medical problem or internal parasites could be to blame, particularly if your cat has just begun to chew when he never did before. Some cats develop these behaviors seemingly from nowhere and others appear to have been born with the desire to eat strange materials. Other cats might be compensating for something they feel they have been missing from the time they were kittens.

Play is Important!

Make sure you set aside time to play with your cat every day. Once a week or every now and then is not enough, particularly for a young or rambunctious cat. Several short play sessions a day are better than one and will keep your cat's mind occupied throughout the day.

Touching is a Good Thing

It's a good idea to acclimate your cat to being petted over his entire body so that you can feel if there is anything wrong with your cat. A friend of mine recently discovered that her cat had a tumor on her belly, but since my friend's cat never let her pet down there, my friend wasn't able to detect it. The veterinarian felt it when carrying the cat to be weighed. So, being able to touch your cat everywhere is important and could even save his life someday.

For example, if your cat was taken from his mother at a very early age or if he was a late suckler, the need to suckle can be transferred to other objects and materials later in life. If your cat likes to chew on, say, your blankets, but seems to be doing more sucking than chewing and he kneads with his paws at the same time and purrs, this is a behavior stemming from kittenhood. It is usually harmless and, unless you can't

Get your cat used to being petted all over so you are always able to recognize changes in his body or fur.

Practical Solutions to Pesky Problems

Holiday Safety

If your cat likes to chew, be extra careful around the holidays. There are many new items around the house this time of the year that can cause kitty great harm. Your cat may be intrigued by lit candles, or decide to play with glass ornaments dangling from the Christmas tree. Make sure you are careful with ribbons, bows, scissors, tinsel, and any small objects a cat or kitten can swallow. Anything breakable or toxic (such as Poinsettia plants) should also be kept out of your cat's reach. Unplug lighted decorations when no one is there to supervise the cat and hide the cords or spray them with a cat-approved bitter substance. If you have many visitors during the holidays, and your cat becomes stressed when people visit, you may want to put your cat in a closed-off room until the company goes home.

Some plants can be dangerous for your cat to eat. Give him his own safe garden of catnip and cat greens to play in.

stand wet blankets, nothing really needs to be done about it. You may want to consider giving your cat his own special blanket or object to suckle on.

However, if this chewing behavior is recent and your cat is an adult, or if he is actually eating and swallowing the materials, something should be done to stop him. Some substances, such as plastic or Styrofoam, can be very dangerous for a cat to eat. As with plants, a non-toxic spray

Your Outta Control Cat

"Cat-proof" your house to help keep your cat from getting hurt.

substance (such as bitter apple) can be used if the cat seems particularly fond of one item. Some materials can be kept away from the cat, but sometimes chewing on materials can be a sign of a behavior-related problem or stress. In this case, simply removing the material or substance won't be enough; you will have to go beneath the surface and find out what is wrong with your cat and determine what is causing this behavior.

The Nip, The Growl, The Bite

Biting can also be a very normal behavior for a cat or kitten. Some cats show affection by offering "love bites" that can range from mild to painful. It is natural for a cat to bite if he feels scared or threatened, as he naturally tries to defend himself. Some cats are also very picky about where you touch them.

On that same note, some cats will let you pet them only for certain periods of time before they have had enough. And how are they

Practical Solutions to Pesky Problems

supposed to let you know they are getting annoyed with the attention? Some cats might just walk away, but others, who are a bit more audacious, will bite your hand and run away. These are not behavioral problems, but normal personality traits for your particular cat.

Litter Box "Accidents"

Litter box mishaps can be cleaned up using baking soda and a paper towel. However, because a lapse in the litter box habit is often a sign that something is wrong, you want to be more thorough in your scrubbing of the area where the cat has been going. Be sure you remove all traces of odor to prevent the cat from wanting to go on that spot again. After blotting away the moisture with a paper towel, pour an enzymatic cleaner into the area to break down the organic matter. Baking soda can be sprinkled on afterward and when the mess

Be careful not to leave things around that your cat could get a hold of and swallow.

is cleaned up, and the lack of odor should prevent the cat from returning. Keep the area covered until it's dry. Try taping something that the cat finds unpleasant over the area, such as double-sided tape or tinfoil. Besides cleaning the area, you can use a carpet deodorizer on a regular basis when vacuuming to cover any surface odors. Using a dust-free litter and placing the box on an easily cleanable surface will help cut down litter tracking and keep the dust from the litter box from filling the air.

If your cat likes to chew on things, make sure electrical cords are not accessible to him.

Safety First

Make sure that you keep you home "cat-proofed" at all times. Secure fireplaces and kerosene heaters with safety screens to keep your cat from getting burned. Cats love to sleep so close to wood-burning stoves that their fur can actually get hot to the touch. It is in your cat's best interest to make sure the cat cannot come into contact or be exposed to hot embers or sparks.

If you live in an older house or apartment, is the paint lead-based? This is a good thing to find out because if your cat chews on this paint, it could kill him. If the paint is chipping and you have the means, repainting should be done as soon as possible.

Practical Solutions to Pesky Problems

Your cat can also get injured in places where he could get inadvertently trapped, such as the dishwasher, the clothes dryer, or the washing machine. Always keep the doors closed and check the appliances before you use them.

Think Ahead

Cats are very curious. To help your cat to stay happy and healthy, learn to anticipate his actions.

Always staying one step ahead of kitty will make your job much easier, whether it is keeping kitty from eating your houseplants or teaching a kitten not to bite. Of course, it takes time to get to know your cat well enough to anticipate his every move in advance, and even then you won't always be able to know everything he is going to do before he does it. Cats are intelligent and are always thinking; therefore, they can be quite unpredictable.

Interacting with your cat on a regular basis and paying attention to him will teach you how to know his behaviors and know when something might upset him. Being in sync with your cat will give you a better hold on the situation if a problem arises, so always try to be one step ahead of your cat. Just keep in mind the few basic rules. Keep it simple, keep it light, and never use force. Always be positive, gentle, and patient, and things will go much more smoothly.

You and Your Cat: Friends for Life

In This Chapter You'll Learn:

✳ Relationship maintenance and communication

✳ How to do a cat massage

✳ How to do a home health exam

✳ How to teach your cat simple tricks

Y ou and your cat are going to be together for a long time. Most cats, particularly those that live indoors, live a good 15 to 18 years or more, provided they receive the proper nutrition, play, interaction, veterinary care, and love. It is important to establish a loving bond with your cat throughout his life and to maintain a good relationship with him. This means being consistent with certain criteria you have established (such as the rules of the household) and dealing with any new issues that crop up as the cat matures and ages (such as incontinence in later years).

Your life with your cat will fall into a comfortable routine and as time progresses you will get to know him and know how he ticks. Therefore, you will be able to tell when something has upset the routine and caused a problem. You will know immediately when something is wrong, even something that is not terribly obvious, and this knowledge will give you a better understanding on how to make things right. This is all part of maintaining the relationship between you and your cat and being your cat's best friend.

Relationship Maintenance and Communication

There are many non-verbal ways to communicate with your cat.

You don't have to be a "pet psychic" to understand your cat. You can communicate with your cat through your knowledge of what he likes and dislikes, as well as through body language. Pet your cat often and spend some quality time grooming him every day. You can also talk to your cat or read to him. He might not understand the words, but the sound of your soothing voice is a good way to develop a bond with your cat. Always talk to your cat softly and keep the lines of communication open. Cats love to be cooed at and spoken to softly. Set aside time each day and carry on a "gab session" with your cat that includes lots of petting, quality time, and play.

Communicating with your feline isn't really difficult at all. "But I don't speak cat," you might say. Sure you do, you're just not aware of it. Every time your cat swishes his tail and you back away, you are communicating. This is part of learning to know your cat, knowing what

As time passes and you spend quality time together, your relationship with your cat will continue to grow.

You and Your Cat: Friends for Life

he thinks, and knowing how he reacts to various stimuli in his environment. In essence, you are interpreting his body language.

This is also how cats communicate with each other. Cats do not verbally communicate with each another as they do with humans. If they fight together, they growl, but they do not carry on verbal conversations. Yet, your cat will sometimes "talk" to you, won't he? You know when he wants to eat because he stares at you and meows. Some cats will even "talk" to you when you come home.

Since you know that communicating with your cat is important, make a point to learn how to connect by learning what techniques your cat uses with you and what he wants with each "word" his body or his voice relays. This will create a stronger bond between you and your cat, and it will make for a more satisfying relationship overall.

Giving your pet a massage is fun and it can also relieve stress in both you and your cat.

Your Outta Control Cat

Make the Most of Your Cat's Massage

Massaging your cat has more benefits than you might think. Stress relief and lowered blood pressure are only a few of the benefits for both you and your cat. Massage is also a way to bond to your cat, and it can be used as physical therapy for arthritic and older cats. If your cat has a special medical condition, consult your veterinarian before you start massaging your feline friend.

Cat Massage

You love getting a massage, right? What makes you think your cat wouldn't? There are numerous benefits of massage for both you and the cat. Giving your cat a massage will not only relieve stress in your cat, but it can lower your blood pressure as well.

Even ornery cats love massages, as long as it is done when the cat is in the mood to be pet and rubbed. A cat will usually let you know when he has had enough either by suddenly scratching, biting, or walking away. You don't want to invoke this reaction, however, so don't force the issue if your cat seems as though he's had enough.

How to Give Your Cat a Massage

Giving a cat a massage involves a little more than a simple petting. Start by petting the cat gently all over. Feel through his fur and all around, petting him the way he likes best. Starting with the head, scratch behind the ears, under the chin, and anywhere else that is pleasant for him. Using your thumbs, carefully rub the cat in light, slow, circular motions. Working at the animal's muscles, move your way down to the neck, back, legs, and paws. Your cat may enjoy the massage so much that he may roll over for you to rub his belly. Make sure you work the kinks out of the leg muscles. Be careful of any sensitive areas (such as sore spots or surgery areas), areas that might invoke a bad reaction (such as belly or tail), or any injured areas.

Your Health Care Commitment

Every cat owner should perform a home health exam on his or her cat (or cats) periodically. Giving your cat the once-over to check for possible ailments or injuries is just one way to keep your cat healthy throughout his lifetime. Home health exams are not difficult to do and only take a short period of time, but they can save your cat's life or at least save him discomfort if anything should be wrong. If you start these sessions when your cat is a kitten and perform them once every few weeks or even once a month, your cat should grow to enjoy the attention.

This is the beginning of a wonderful start to your relationship with your cat. Home health exams can be a great measure in assuring your cat's

By becoming aware of your cat's normal condition, you will be able to keep his minor problems from turning into major ones.

Your Outta Control Cat

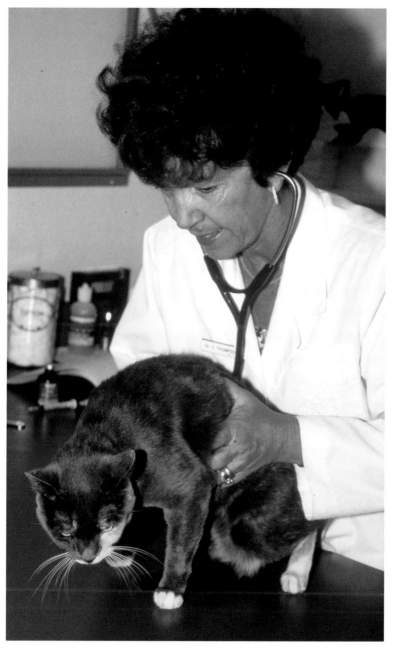

In addition to regular visits to the veterinarian, you should give your cat periodical home health exams.

You and Your Cat: Friends for Life

continued health, as well as become another bonding technique to bring the two of you closer together. Catching ailments before they become a problem is the first step in assuring your cat's continued health, and a home health exam is one way to do this.

How to do a Home Health Exam

Start your exam by stepping back and looking at your cat. Ask yourself the following questions: Has the cat been behaving and acting normally? Is he walking with the proper gait? Is his balance as it should be? Any noticeable changes should be immediately brought to the attention of your veterinarian.

Next, start the physical part of the exam, and use food treats and lots of praise as the reward. Keep your cat calm throughout the exam. If at any time he begins to become agitated, it is best to stop

Home exams are an important part of maintaining your cat's health and they only take a few minutes.

Your Outta Control Cat

Checking your cat's eyes is one important part of the home health exam. They should be bright and clean.

You and Your Cat: Friends for Life

and continue another time when he has relaxed. Negative associations will only make future exams more difficult on you, as well as your cat.

The Eyes

Start the exam by looking at your cat's eyes. They should be bright, clear, and free of excessive discharge. A small amount of clear discharge may be normal, but thick, dark discharge may be the sign of a problem, such as a blocked tear duct or conjunctivitis, and should be brought to the attention of your veterinarian. If your cat bumps into things or seems to have trouble deciphering distances, you will want your veterinarian to check his eyesight.

Check the lenses of your cat's eyes. Do they seem normal? Cloudiness may be the sign of cataracts. Redness or discharge around the area of the lids may mean conjunctivitis.

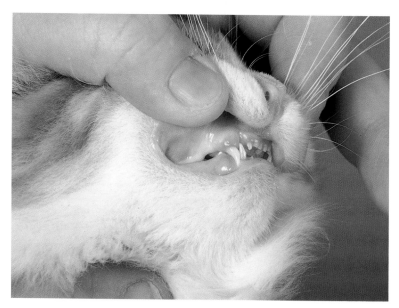

Be gentle when trying to look in your cat's mouth, because most felines do not like to have their mouths opened.

Your Outta Control Cat

Normal Vital Signs

When you do a home health exam, you can check your cat's heart rate. You can feel the pulse by gently pressing right behind the cat's left front leg over the chest area. A normal heart rate should run between 120 to 220 beats per minute. (The more relaxed the cat is, the lower his heart rate will be.) Respiration should be even and barely visible (unless the cat is purring). Open-mouth breathing, holding the head extended while breathing, or excessive chest movement while breathing is abnormal in cats and should be checked by a veterinarian.

The Ears

Examine the ears next. They should be clean and pink, not red or swollen. A foul odor is the sign of an ear infection. If the ears look dirty or if the cat scratches at them continually, ear mites may be present.

The Mouth

Looking into your cat's mouth will take a bit more effort and is an activity that you should start while the cat is young in order to acclimate him to it. Most cats resist having their mouths opened, and you will need to be easy and gentle. Place your hand over the cat's head and, using your thumb and middle finger, press lightly on either side of the cat's mouth until it opens. The gums should be pink, not white, bluish, or yellow. Lifting one lip carefully, press on the gums. They should turn white at your touch and then within seconds be restored to their natural color. There should be no foul odor from the mouth. An odor can indicate the presence of an infection or even kidney or digestive problems. Teeth should be white, not yellow or brown, but will vary according to the cat's age.

Brushing your cat's teeth using a pet toothpaste (ask your veterinarian to recommend a brand) or a baking soda and water mixture is a good

You and Your Cat: Friends for Life

idea, because excess tartar can build on your cat's teeth just like on your own. Cats also develop dental disease, and teeth cleanings at the veterinarian can be expensive. Do not use toothpastes made for humans as they may make a cat ill.

The Body

Starting at the neck and throat, feel down the sides of your cat's body. Feel for any lumps or sore spots either on the skin or under the skin. Do a fat-cat check. If you can't feel your pet's ribs, it may be time for a diet. On the other hand, if the ribs are sticking out or are more prominent than normal, the cat is losing weight. This could be the indication of a serious health problem.

Next, gently pull the skin up on your cat's neck. The skin should fall right back into place when released. If the skin remains, your pet may be dehydrated. Sift your fingers through your cat's coat. Look for fleas or any sign of parasites. Flea dirt resembles tiny specks of pepper and turns red when dampened.

Feel along your cat's legs and paws, and feel between the toes as well. Check for any sign of swelling, pain, lumps, or stiffness. Last, look at the cat's anal area for any excess discharge or redness. Tapeworms are occasionally visible and resemble small bits of rice. However, it is still good practice to have your cat's stool checked for internal parasites whenever he visits the veterinarian.

A cat's anal sacs are located on either side of the anus. If an anal sac gets impacted it can cause severe irritation. If your cat is "scooting" his hind end along the floor or licking excessively at the anal area, have a veterinarian check the cat for impaction.

It seems like doing all this will take a considerable amount of time, but

Your Outta Control Cat

really once you are used to doing it, it will take only a few minutes. In the long run, both you and your cat will find the benefits.

Teaching Your Old (or New) Cat New Tricks

Relationship maintenance does not have to be boring. It does not have to involve simply watching how your cat walks or whether he eats properly every day. Part of keeping your cat happy and healthy also involves keeping him interested in his life. A bored cat will sit around just wanting to eat and sleep and may grow overweight and develop health or behavioral problems. Playing with your cat is one way to assure this doesn't happen, but you can go beyond that. Why not teach your cat tricks? It's fun, it will keep you involved in your cat's life, keep your cat from getting bored, and will also help bond the two of you together.

Instead of allowing your cat to get bored and develop behavioral problems, play with him and teach him tricks.

You and Your Cat: Friends for Life

Teach your cat one trick at a time so he doesn't get confused.

Your Outta Control Cat

Clickers

Some cats can learn to do tricks through means of an external stimulus, such as hearing a particular sound. Professional trainers will often use clickers in association with a food reward to tell the cat "it's time to do your trick now" or to reinforce a behavior.

A clicker is a small plastic or metal device held in the hand that will make a clicking noise when pressed. A series of actions can be taught using this method. For example, you can train the cat to come when he hears the click, and then build on this simple learned command. If you use this method, your cat will learn to perform the designated trick every time he hears the click.

There are several tricks you can start with that are quite easy, but you can teach your cat anything you want. To start, try the simple things first, and remember: the younger the cat is, the easier he will be to train. Never forget patience and understanding. Use the reward system for trick

When teaching your cat to beg, make sure he is paying attention and then be patient as he learns the trick.

You and Your Cat: Friends for Life

Begging and fetching are two tricks that almost any cat can learn.

training, and never be negative in any way. Here, we'll show you how to teach your cat to beg and fetch. They are two of the simplest tricks to learn because they involve acting upon your cat's innate behaviors.

Starting Out

The first factor in teaching tricks is to have the utmost patience. Cats are not dogs and they do not learn in the same manner as dogs. Dogs can be taught to follow commands on praise alone, but with cats you will need to use a food reward plus the praise. Find out what your cat's favorite treat is. Try to use something small and easy to hand out a tiny bit at a time. Bits of dried liver can be bought at pet stores and cats love them. Use the treat as the reward. Make sure that you only use these treats for training. Don't give them to your cat at any other time. Pick one trick and teach only that one trick until the cat has learned it well. You don't want to confuse your cat by trying to teach him too many tricks at once.

To keep your cat from getting confused, teach only one trick at a time.

Cats are very intelligent, love to play, and are more than capable of learning tricks.

What Tricks Can My Cat Learn?

You can teach your cat all kinds of tricks (both simple and complex), depending on how much time and energy you wish to spend in training, and the overall health and age of your cat. Some older cats will not be interested in or capable of learning the more physically demanding tricks. Here are a few tricks you can teach your cat.

* Come when called.
* Go to a particular location.
* Jump onto an object (such as a chair, bookshelf, or your shoulder).
* Roll over.
* Leap from one designated area to another.

Use your imagination, and you can come up with many tricks for your cat to perform. Using the cat's innate abilities, such as "catching" prey or leaping from high locations, will make training easier. Another great book on this subject is *Cat Training in 10 Minutes* by Miriam Fields-Babineau (TFH Publications, 2003).

Start training time when your cat is awake and when he is most likely to be receptive to your commands.

Teaching Your Cat to Beg

To teach your cat how to beg, hold the treat between your fingers and show it to him. Make sure he knows the treat is in your hand and smells it. But do not give it to him yet. Raise your hand slowly above his head, making him follow and sit up on his haunches. When he starts to reach for the treat, say "Beg," and hand him the treat. Repeat this several times. At the point when you want him to learn the trick, hand him the treat each time. Do this every day, and then slowly try just giving the

Teaching a cat tricks usually involves only treats and lots of patience.

Your Outta Control Cat

Learning to fetch can be fun and provide good exercise for your cat.

command, but keep the treat in your hand. See if the cat sits up. If he does, have a treat and lots of praise ready. If the cat does not sit up, then start the training session over again. Most cats get it after several weeks if you are diligent and work with them daily. Keep the training sessions short, (about five to ten minutes a day) so your cat does not become bored (or overfed!).

Teaching Your Cat to Fetch

Teaching a cat to fetch is always a fun trick. My cat, Pounce, once taught himself to fetch a small ball. Most cats need more encouragement than simply a love of play, however, and this is where your food reward will come in handy.

The first step in teaching a cat to fetch is to use a toy the cat loves and will want to chase. Make sure you use a ball or a round object that can't be eaten, swallowed, or chewed up. A ball that has grooves or holes is good because it will be easier for your cat to pick up and bring back to you.

Rub the toy in catnip and show it to your cat. When the toy is covered in the catnip smell (you can use catnip leaves or catnip spray found in pet shops), show it to the cat, make sure he wants it, and toss it a few feet away. When the cat runs to retrieve the toy, follow him and take the toy once he has "caught" it. Praise him and tell him that he's a good kitty as you take the toy. Return to where you were originally standing and make sure that the cat follows you. Once you have the cat's attention, toss the ball a little further and repeat the process.

You might want to add verbal commands such as saying, "Fetch," and perhaps give the cat a very tiny food reward. If you keep it fun and don't make the sessions to long or too heavy, eventually you might find your cat bringing the toy back to you so you can throw it again.

Teaching Your Cat to Walk on a Leash

I have known people who have walked their cats on leashes, and this can be a great way for your indoor cat to get some fresh air. It is also a fantastic bonding tool. Don't, however, expect your cat to walk on a leash like a dog would. The cat might follow along, but he won't heel at your side. It only takes a few simple steps to teach your cat to walk on a leash and, again, the younger the cat is when you start the training, the easier the training will be.

You first need to get your cat used to the harness. (Always use a cat harness and not a collar to walk your cat. A collar can slip and choke your cat.) Hook your cat into the harness and let him get used to it. Be sure to give him lots of food rewards and praise. You might want to do this daily for a week or so until he is comfortable wearing the harness around the house.

Cats can be taught to walk on a leash, an activity that can be both fun and provide needed exercise.

Next, hook a light leash onto the harness and let the cat drag the leash around the house for a few days or weeks, until he becomes used to the weight and feel of it.

Whenever your cat is comfortable, start "walking" your cat around the house. Use food to lure him to walk with you and also let him go where he wants. Never force him into anything.

When the cat is accustomed to walking around the house, try taking him into the yard and see how he reacts. If he is terribly frightened, bring him back inside. This training sometimes doesn't work as well with an older cat that has always been an indoor cat. In fact, unless there's a very specific reason, you shouldn't leash-train an older cat that has never been outside and has no desire to go out, particularly if the cat is shy. The experience could make the cat worse.

You and Your Cat: Friends for Life

Take time to show your pet how much you love him. Be patient and your outta control cat might very well turn into your best friend.

Once your cat is comfortable walking around the yard, try taking him to other places, like on a sidewalk, but avoid areas of heavy traffic (foot or vehicle) until he is completely comfortable. Remember to take each step gradually, use praise and rewards, and eventually you might have a cat walking alongside you as you take your daily walk.

Time is Love

All the remedies, training, and care outlined in this book might seem like a lot of work. Many people think owning a cat simply means acquiring the cat, placing him in the home with a litter box, and feeding him once or twice a day. There is much, much more to it than that. Take the time to truly know and love your cat. Play with him, watch him, and talk to him. Love your cat, and he will love you right back.

Resources

Magazines

ASPCA Animal Watch
424 East 92nd Street
New York, NY 10128-6804
(212) 876-7700
www.aspca.org
E-mail: communications@
aspca.org

Cat Fancy
Subscription Department
P.O. Box 53264
Boulder, CO 80322-3264
(800) 365-4421
www.catfancy.com
E-mail: fancy@neodata.com

Cats & Kittens
Pet Publishing, Inc.
7-L Dundas Circle
Greensboro, NC 27407
336.292.4047
Fax: 336.292.4272
www.catsandkittens.com
E-mail: cksubscriptions@petpub-
lishing.com

Your Cat Magazine
1716 Locust Street
Des Moines, IA 50309

Cat clubs and Societies

American Association of Cat Enthusiasts (AACE)
P.O. Box 213
Pine Brook, NJ 07058
(973) 335-6717
Fax: (973) 334-5834
www.aaceinc.org
E-mail: info@aaeinc.org

American Cat Fanciers Association (ACFA)
P.O Box 1949
Nixa, MO 65714-1949
(417) 725-1530

Fax: (417) 725-1533
www.acfacat.com
E-mail: mcats@bellsouth.net

The Cat Fanciers' Association, Inc.(CFA)
P.O. Box 1005
Manasquan, NJ 08736-0805.
Phone: (732) 528-9797
Fax: (732) 528-7391
www.cfainc.org/
E-mail: cfa@cfainc.org

The International Cat Association (TICA)
P.O. Box 2684
Harlingen, TX 78551
(956) 428-8046
Fax: (956) 428-8047
www.tica.org
E-mail: ticaeo@xanadu2.net

Traditional and Classic Cat International (TCCI)
10289 Vista Point Loop
Penn Valley, CA 95946
www.tccat.org
E-mail: tccat@tccat.org

Web Resources

Cat Fanciers website
www.fanciers.com

Internet Cat Club
www.netcat.org

The Daily Cat
www.thedailycat.com

Pet adopathon
www.petadoptathon.com

Healthypet
www.healthypet.com

Vetquest
www.vetquest.com

Rescue and Adoption Organizations

Alley Cat Allies
1801 Belmont Road NW, Suite 201
Washington, DC 20009
(202) 667-3630
Fax: (202) 667-3640
www.alleycat.org

The American Society for the Prevention of Cruelty to Animals
424 East 92nd Street
New York, NY 10128-6801
(212) 876-7700
www.aspca.org
E-mail: information@aspca.org

Best Friends Animal Sanctuary
5001 Angel Canyon Road
Kanab, UT 84741-5001
Phone: (435) 644-2001
Fax: (435) 644-2078
www.bestfriends.org
e-mail: info@bestfriends.org

Feral Cat Coalition
9528 Miramar Road, PMB 160
San Diego, CA 92126
(619) 497-1599
www.feralcat.com
e-mail: rsavage@feralcat.com

The Humane Society of the United States (HSUS)
Companion Animals Section
2100 L Street, NW
Washington, DC 20037
(202)- 452-1100
www.hsus.org

North Shore Animal League America
25 Davis Avenue
Port Washington, NJ 11050
(516) 883-7575
www.nsal.org
E-mail: nsal1@aol.com

Pet Finder
www.petfinder.org
Petfinder.com is an online, searchable database of over 100,000 animals that need homes from over 5,000 animal shelters and adoption organizations across the USA and Canada. Organizations maintain their own home pages and available pet database. Launched in 1996, Petfinder was the first site of its kind and is today the largest single force introducing homeless pets with new families. Petfinder.com was responsible for over a half million adoptions last year!

Pet Sitters

Pet Sitters International
201 East King Street
King, NC 27021-9161
Phone: (336)-983-9222
FAX (336)-983-5266
www.petsit.com

National Association of Professional Pet Sitters
17000 Commerce Parkway, Suite C
Mt. Laurel, NJ 08054
(800) 296-PETS or (856) 439-0324
Fax: (856) 439-0525
www.petsitters.org
E-mail: napps@ahint.com

Emergency Resources

Animal Poison Hotline
(888) 2320-8870

ASPCA Animal Poison Control Center
(888) 426-4435
www.aspca.org

Index

Photos:

Joan Balzarini: 32, 34, 42, 45, 68, 73, 135, 145
Linda Beatie: 30, 66
Richard K Blackmon: 50, 109, 117
Jacquie DeLillo: 86
Isabelle Francais: 7, 8, 15, 16, 20, 21, 23, 33, 35, 37-41, 43, 46, 49, 51, 55, 58, 59, 61, 67, 74, 76, 77, 81, 93, 94, 96, 100, 101, 107, 108, 110, 114, 116, 121, 122, 127, 128, 130, 131, 134, 136, 137, 141-143, 146, 148
Keri Johnson: 84
A. D. Lawrence: 47
Stuart Levine: 62
Gillian Lisle: 11, 18, 19, 88, 144, 152
Robert Pearcy: 3, 6, 13, 22, 24, 26, 36, 56, 63, 70, 71, 79, 82, 85, 90, 97, 99, 103-106, 113, 115, 119, 123-126
Vince Serbin: 48, 64, 78, 120
Lara Stern: 92, 112, 138
Linda Sturdy: 9, 10, 25, 29, 31, 54, 95, 102, 151
Karen Taylor: 89
John Tyson: 27, 80, 149
Kelli Wilkins: 132